STAND OUT

Evidence-Based Learning for College and Career Readiness

1

THIRD EDITION

WORKBOOK

ROB JENKINS

STACI JOHNSON

T0308641

NATIONAL GEOGRAPHIC LEARNING | CENGAGE Learning®

Braulio Jeronimo

Australia • Brazil • Mexico • Singapore • United Kingdom • United States

NATIONAL GEOGRAPHIC LEARNING | CENGAGE Learning

Stand Out 1: Evidence-Based Learning for College and Career Readiness, Workbook
Third Edition
Rob Jenkins and Staci Johnson

Publisher: Sherrise Roehr
Executive Editor: Sarah Kenney
Senior Development Editor: Margarita Matte
Assistant Editor: Patricia Giunta
Director of Global Marketing: Ian Martin
Executive Marketing Manager: Ben Rivera
Product Marketing Manager: Dalia Bravo
Media Researcher: Leila Hishmeh
Director of Content and Media Production: Michael Burggren
Production Manager: Daisy Sosa
Senior Print Buyer: Mary Beth Hennebury
Cover and Interior Designer: Brenda Carmichael
Composition: Lumina
Cover Image: Portra Images/Getty Images
Bottom Images: (Left to Right) Jay B Sauceda/ Getty Images; Tripod/Getty Images; Portra Images/Getty Images; James Porter/ Getty Images; Mark Edward Atkinson/ Tracey Lee/Getty Images; Hero Images/ Getty Images; Jade/Getty Images; Seth Joel/ Getty Images; LWA/Larry Williams/ Getty Images; Dimitri Otis/Getty Images

Work Book
ISBN 13: 978-1-305-65542-3

National Geographic Learning/Cengage Learning
20 Channel Center Street
Boston, MA 02210
USA

Cengage Learning is a leading provider of customized learning solutions with office locations around the globe, including Singapore, the United Kingdom, Australia, Mexico, Brazil and Japan. Locate our local office at:
international.cengage.com/region

Visit National Geographic Learning online at **NGL.Cengage.com**
Visit our corporate website at **www.cengage.com**

Printed in China by RRD
Print Number: 13 Print Year: 2023

CONTENTS

TO THE TEACHER

ABOUT THE SERIES

The **Stand Out** series is designed to facilitate *active* learning within life-skill settings that leads students to career and academic pathways. Each student book and its supplemental components in the six-level series expose students to competency areas most useful and essential for newcomers, with careful treatment of level-appropriate but challenging materials. Students grow academically by developing essential literacy and critical thinking skills that will help them find personal success in a changing and dynamic world.

STAND OUT WORKBOOK

The **Stand Out Workbook** is designed to provide additional practice for learners to reinforce what they learned in each student book lesson. It can be used as homework or as a supplement to the lesson in the classroom. Each lesson in **Stand Out** is driven by a life-skill objective and supported by vocabulary and grammar. Students are not expected to master or acquire vocabulary and grammar completely after being exposed to it just one time, hence the need for additional practice. The lessons in the student book are three pages long and each supporting workbook lesson is also three pages long. The workbook lessons correlate directly with the student book lessons.

The **Stand Out Workbook** establishes a link to new content by providing the essential vocabulary introduced in the books in a way that also promotes critical thinking skills. Promoting critical thinking skills is essential for students to become independent lifelong learners. About half of the three-page practice is grammar focused where students are given a chart with notes, study how the grammar facilitates communication, and gain additional needed confidence through practice.

HOW TO USE THE STAND OUT WORKBOOK

The workbook can be used in the following ways:

1. The activities in the workbook can be used as additional practice during class to reinforce one or more practice activities in the student book.
2. The activities in the workbook can be assigned as homework. This is often a good way to reinforce what students have learned. The skills, vocabulary, and structures may not transfer into long-term memory after the lesson, so reinforcing the lesson after a short period of time away can be very helpful. Additionally, teachers can also review the homework at the beginning of each class, giving students another opportunity to be exposed to the information. Reviewing the homework is also a good strategy for the *Warm-up/Review* portion of the lesson and can be used in place of the one proposed in the **Stand Out Lesson Planner**.
3. The **Stand Out Workbook** can be used as a tool in the flipped classroom. In flipped classrooms, students prepare for lessons away from class before they are presented. Since the **Stand Out Workbook** introduces much of the vocabulary and grammar for each lesson, it is ideal for incorporating this approach.

ADDITIONAL PRACTICE

The **Stand Out** series is a comprehensive one-stop for all student needs. There is no need to look any further than the resources offered. Additional practice is available through the online workbook, which is different from the print workbook. There are also hundreds of multi-level worksheets available online. Please visit ngl.cengage.com/so3 to get easy access to all resources.

PRE-UNIT

LESSON 1 Hello!

GOAL ■ Greet people

A. Look at the picture. Read about Lien.

Lien is a student at Johnson Adult School. She is a good student. Mario is her friend. He is a student, too. Lien and Mario go to school at night. Mr. Serna is the teacher in the class.

B. Draw lines to match information.

Lien	teacher
Mario	friend
Mr. Serna	student

C. Read the conversation.

Roberto: Hi. I'm Roberto. What's your name?

Gabriela: My name is Gabriela.

Roberto: Welcome to our class.

Gabriela: Thank you.

Roberto: Our teacher is Miss Jones.

D. Write the names of four students in your class.

	What's Your Name?
1.	
2.	
3.	
4.	

E. Read the chart.

The Verb *Be* in Greetings				
Greeting	**Subject**	***Be***	**Your name**	**Example sentence**
hi hello	I	am	Hans Maria	Hi. I **am** Hans. (*I'**m** Hans.*)
	my name	is		Hello. My name **is** Maria. (*Hello. My name'**s** Maria.*)

F. Read the information.

Students in My Class	
1. Andrew	2. Esmeralda
3. Eva	4. Gabriela
5. Gilberto	6. Ivan
7. Roberto	8. Tri

G. Write sentences about Exercise F.

1. My name is Andrew.
2. ____________
3. ____________
4. ____________
5. ____________
6. ____________
7. ____________
8. ____________

H. Rewrite the sentences using the contracted form of *I am*.

1. I am Andrew. I'm Andrew.
2. I am Esmeralda. ____________
3. I am Eva. ____________
4. I am Gabriela. ____________
5. I am Gilberto. ____________
6. I am Ivan. ____________
7. I am Roberto. ____________
8. I am Tri. ____________

I. Write a conversation.

You: Hello.

Partner: ____________

You: ____________

Partner: ____________

PRE-UNIT

LESSON 2 # What's your number?

GOAL ■ Say and write numbers

A. Look at the information and write it under the pictures below.

2929 W. Beach	New Town	714-555-2211	Marie	90691

Name: Gilberto
Address:
City: Alton
State: California
Zip Code:
Phone:

Name:
Address: 72451 Harbor
City:
State: California
Zip Code: 92691
Phone: 949-555-3765

B. Complete the sentences about Gilberto.

1. Gilberto's address is ______________________________.
2. His phone number is ______________________________.
3. His zip code is ______________________________.

C. Write sentences about Marie.

1. Marie's address is ______________________________.
2. ______________________________.
3. ______________________________.

D. Read the class list and complete the sentences.

Class List		
Name	**Phone number**	**Address**
Gabriela	(401) 555-7248	14 Main Street
Roberto	(619) 555-6903	2315 Wilshire Place
Eva	(401) 555-3534	333 Western Circle
Tri	(562) 555-2876	7267 Broadway

1. My name's Gabriela. My address is 14 Main Street.
2. My name's Roberto. My phone number is ______________________.
3. I'm Eva. My address is ______________________.
4. I'm Tri. My phone number is ______________________.
5. I'm Gabriela. My phone number is ______________________.
6. My name's ______________________. My phone number is (401) 555-3534.
7. My name's ______________________. My address is 2315 Wilshire Place.
8. I'm ______________________. My phone number is (401) 555-7248.

E. Read the chart.

It is (It's)			
Subject	***Be***	**Information**	**Example sentence**
It The address The phone number	is	265 Main Street.	It's 265 Main Street.
		265 Main Street.	The address is 265 Main Street.
		555-1234.	The phone number is 555-1234.

F. Rewrite the sentences with *It's*.

1. The phone number is 555-3755. It's 555-3755. ______
2. The address is 14 Main Street. ______
3. The phone number is 555-2876. ______
4. It is 555-2933. ______
5. It is 25821 West Birch Street. ______
6. It is 555-9912. ______
7. It is 373 Cypress Ave. ______
8. The phone number is 555-9090. ______

G. With a partner, turn the sentences in Exercise F into questions and answers. Take turns asking and answering the questions.

Student A: What's the phone number?

Student B: It's 555-3755.

H. Read the class list in Exercise D again. Answer the questions with sentences.

1. What's Eva's address? It's 333 Western Circle. ______
2. What's Eva's phone number? ______
3. What's Tri's phone number? ______
4. What's Roberto's phone number? ______
5. What's Gabriela's address? ______
6. What's Roberto's address? ______

I. Answer the questions with *It's*.

1. What's your address? ______
2. What's your phone number? ______
3. What's a friend's address? ______
4. What's a friend's phone number? ______

PRE-UNIT

LESSON 3 Classroom talk

GOAL ■ Follow instructions

A. Label the picture with words from the box.

board	desks	teacher
book	student	window

B. Complete sentences about the words in Exercise A.

1. The teacher writes on the ________________.
2. Students sit at ________________.
3. The teacher talks to a ________________.
4. She asks students to open their ________________.
5. The students listen to the ________________.
6. Please open the ________________. It is hot inside.

C. Read the chart.

Imperatives			
Subject	Verb	Information	Example sentence
~~You~~	stand up		**Stand up.**
~~You~~	sit down		**Sit down.**
~~You~~	take out	a piece of paper	**Take out** a piece of paper.
~~You~~	open	the book	**Open** the book.
~~You~~	listen to	the teacher	**Listen** to the teacher.
~~You~~	write	your name	**Write** your name.
~~You~~	help	a student	**Help** a student.
~~You~~	read	a book	**Read** a book.

D. Circle the correct word or words.

1. ____________.	(Stand up)	Stands up	stood up
2. ____________ your books.	open	opens	Open
3. ____________ the paper.	Reads	reading	Read
4. ____________ the teacher.	Listen to	listens to	Listens to
5. ____________ your name.	Open	sit down	Write
6. ____________ a piece of paper.	Take out	open	Listen
7. ____________ a student.	Stand up	Help	Sit down
8. ____________.	stands up	Sit down	Sits down

E. Look at the pictures. Write the action verb.

1.

open

2.

3.

4.
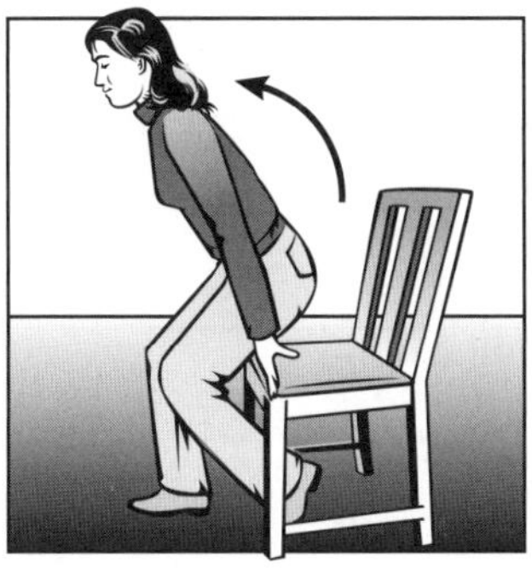

5.
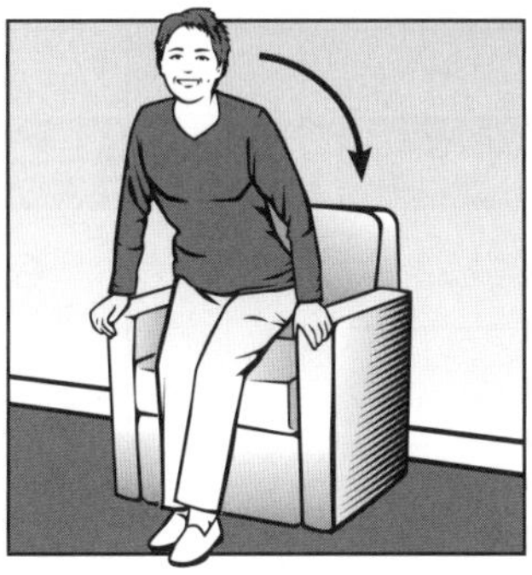

6.

7.

8.

UNIT 1

LESSON 1 Where are you from?

GOAL ■ Ask for and give personal information

A. Read the identification cards and complete the chart.

1

Personal Identification

Kim, Henry

Last First

Bangkok, Thailand

City Country

2

Personal Identification

Ito, Takashi

Last First

Tokyo, Japan

City Country

3

Personal Identification

Conti, Antonio

Last First

Parma, Italy

City Country

4

Personal Identification

Gutierrez, Marco

Last First

Mexico City, Mexico

City Country

First Name	Last Name	City	Country
1. *Henry*			
2.			
3.			
4.			

B. Answer the questions about the information in Exercise A.

1. Where is Henry from? ______________________
2. What is Marco's last name? ______________________
3. Where is Antonio from? ______________________
4. What is Mr. Ito's first name? ______________________

C. Look at the information in the box and complete the chart.

married	33 years old	divorced
single	Russia	15
75 years old	England	China

Marital status	Age	Country

D. Read the chart.

Simple Present: *Be*			
Subject	***Be***	**Information**	**Example sentence**
I	am	43 years old single from Argentina from Russia married	I **am** 43 years old. (***I'm*** *43 years old.*)
He She	is		He **is** single. (Roberto **is** single.) She **is** from Argentina.
We You They	are		We **are** single. You **are** married. They **are** from Russia.

E. Write *am, is,* or *are.*

1. She ___is___ from San Diego.
2. We ________ 35 years old.
3. They ________ from Chicago.
4. I ________ divorced.
5. You ________ married.
6. He ________ 12 years old.
7. John ________ from Honduras.
8. Pedro and Maria ________ married.
9. Jennifer and I ________ from the U.S.
10. Anabel ________ divorced.
11. The students ________ from Cuba.
12. The teacher ________ from Canada.

F. Circle the correct answers.

1. Where are you from?
   - (a.) I am from China.
   - b. I'm China.
   - c. I are from China.
2. How old is Roberto?
   - a. He am 33 years old.
   - b. He are 33 years old.
   - c. He is 33 years old.
3. Are they single, married, or divorced?
   - a. They are married.
   - b. They is married.
   - c. They am married.
4. Where are Melissa and Henry from?
   - a. Melissa are from the United States and Henry are from Korea.
   - b. Melissa are from the United States and Henry is from Korea.
   - c. Melisa is from the United States and Henry is from Korea.
5. How old are Aaron and Rob?
   - a. Aaron is 60 and Rob are 50.
   - b. Aaron and Rob are 50.
   - c. Aaron and Rob is 60.

G. Use the chart to make up sentences to say to a partner.

EXAMPLE: Margarita and Nathan are 35 years old.

Name	Marital status	Age	Country
Margarita	married	35	Guatemala
Nathan	single	35	United States
Caspar	single	45	Guatemala

H. Write sentences about you.

1. (marital status) I ________________________________.
2. (age) I ________________________________.
3. (country) I ________________________________.

LESSON 2 What does he look like?

GOAL ■ Describe people

A. Read the identification card and complete the sentences.

1. The address is ______________________________.
2. The city is ______________________________.
3. The zip code is ______________________________.
4. His first name is ______________________________.
5. His last name is ______________________________.

B. Read the identification cards and answer the questions.

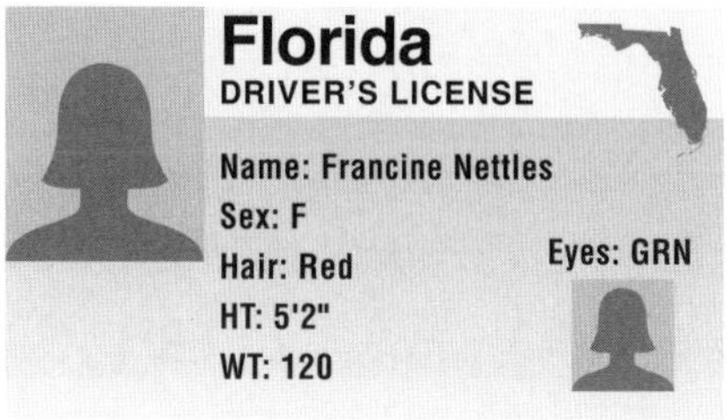

1. What color is Henry's hair? His hair is ______________________________.
2. What color are his eyes? His eyes are ______________________________.
3. What is his height? His height is ______________________________.
4. What is his weight? His weight is ______________________________.

1. What color is Francine's hair? ______________________________.
2. What color are her eyes? ______________________________.
3. What is her height? ______________________________.
4. What is her weight? ______________________________.

C. Complete the sentences using the information. Follow the example.

Name: Kenji
From: Japan
Marital status: single
Hair: black
Eyes: brown

Name: Anya
From: Russia
Marital status: married
Hair: white
Eyes: blue

Name: Mario
From: Mexico
Marital status: divorced
Hair: black
Eyes: brown

Kenji

1. Kenji is from Japan.
2. He is single.
3. His hair is black.
4. His eyes are brown.

Anya

1. ______________________
2. ______________________
3. ______________________
4. ______________________

Mario

1. ______________________
2. ______________________
3. ______________________
4. ______________________

D. Read the charts.

Simple Present: *Have*			
Subject	***Have***	**Information**	**Example sentence**
I, You, We, They	have	black hair brown hair blond hair	I **have** black hair. They **have** brown hair. You **have** blond hair.
He, She, It	has	brown eyes blue eyes	He **has** brown eyes. She **has** blue eyes.

Simple Present: *Be*			
Subject	***Be***	**Information**	**Example sentence**
I	am	5′6″ tall	I **am** 5′6″ tall. (five feet, six inches)
You	are	130 pounds	You **are** 130 pounds.
He, She, It	is	30 years old	She **is** 30 years old.

E. Check (✓) the correct answers.

1. John ___is___ 6 feet tall.	☐ has	☑ is
2. They ___have___ brown hair.	☑ have	☐ are
3. Margarita and Jan ___have___ brown eyes.	☑ have	☐ is
4. You ___have___ 120 pounds.	☑ have	☐ are
5. We ___have___ blue eyes and blond hair.	☑ have	☐ are
6. I ___am___ 25 years old.	☐ have	☒ am
7. She ___is___ 5′ 5″ tall.	☐ has	☑ is
8. I ___have___ brown hair.	☑ have	☐ am
9. He ___has___ black hair.	☑ has	☐ is
10. We ___are___ 32 years old.	☐ have	☐ are

F. Circle the correct answers.

1. Alfredo **has / have** blue eyes.
2. Pauline **has / have** brown hair.
3. We **has / have** green eyes.
4. Pauline and Alfredo **has / have** brown hair.
5. You **has / have** blond hair.
6. I **has / have** black hair.
7. She **am / is / are** from Mexico.
8. The teacher **am / is / are** tall.
9. We **am / is / are** from Nicaragua.
10. You **am / is / are** 42 years old.
11. They **am / is / are** 5′ 2″ tall.
12. I **am / is / are** 24 years old.

G. Use the information below to write sentences.

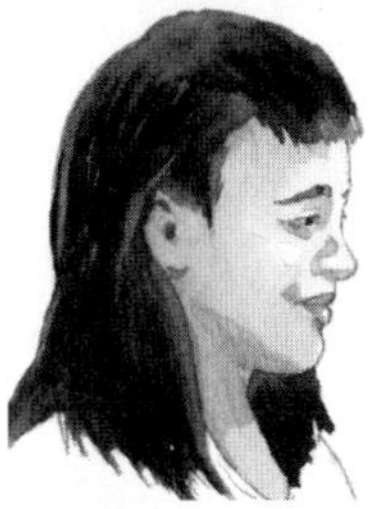
Miriam
straight
brown

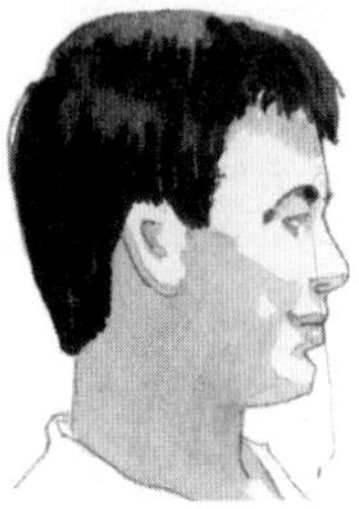
John
short
black

Vincent
wavy
blond

Martha
curly
gray

Nadia
long
red

1. Miriam has straight brown hair.
2. John have the hair short
3. Vincent is blond
4. Martha have eyes gray
5. Nadia have hair long

UNIT 1

LESSON 3 Roberto's family

GOAL ■ Describe family relationships

A. Read the paragraph and complete the family tree.

Ivan and Anya are married. They have one daughter and one son. Irina is the daughter. She is married to Alexi. They have one child. Their daughter's name is Irina. Ivan and Anya's son is Dimitri. Dimitri's wife is Nadia. They have two boys, Vladimir and Ziven.

B. Look at the family tree and circle the correct answer.

1. Ayumi's husband
   a. Kenji
   b. Ikumi
   c. Takuya

2. Akira's wife
   a. Sayuri
   b. Ayumi
   c. Genki

3. Genki's daughter
   a. Ikumi
   b. Yakari
   c. Takayo

4. Kenji's mother
   a. Sayuri
   b. Ayumi
   c. Takuya

C. Read the charts.

Simple Present: *Be*			
Subject	*Be*	Relationship	Example sentence
He She	is	Roberto's brother Roberto's sister	He **is** Roberto's brother. She **is** Roberto's sister.
They	are	Lien's children Lien's parents	They **are** Lien's children. They **are** Lien's parents.

Simple Present: *Have*			
Subject	*Have*	Relationship	Example sentence
I, You, We, They	have	brothers sisters	I **have** three brothers. You **have** one sister. We **have** no brothers. They **have** two sisters.
He She	has		He **has** two sisters. She **has** four brothers.

D. Complete the sentences with the correct form of *be*.

1. Ayumi ____is____ Kenji's mother.
2. Yuuki and Tooru ____have____ Akira's children.
3. Yakari ____is____ Genki's wife.
4. Akira and Genki ____have____ Kenji's brothers.
5. I ____________ Kenji's brother.
6. We ____________ Takuya's children.

E. Complete the sentences with *have* or *has*.

1. Kenji ____has____ two brothers.
2. Tooru ____________ one brother.
3. Yuuki ____________ one aunt.
4. Takuya and Ayumi ____________ three grandchildren.
5. Ikumi, Yukki, and Tooru ____________ three aunts and uncles.
6. We ____________ four children.

F. Read the paragraphs.

I am Olivia. I am Leonel's daughter. I have three brothers and one sister.

Kenji is single. He is Takuya's son. He has two brothers.

G. Write your own paragraph.

I am ____

____

____

____

____

LESSON 4 I like sports and music

GOAL ■ Express preferences

watch

A. Check your preferences for your free time.

☑ animals	☐ homework	☑ shopping
☐ books	☑ movies	☐ sports
☐ computers	☐ museums	☐ studying
☐ exercise	☑ music	☑ time with friends
☑ family time	☐ parks	☑ TV
☐ games	☑ restaurants	☐ video games

B. Write sentences about what you like.

1. I like tha animals.
2. You likes see Movies.
3. She like lisenit to music.
4. he like eat in restaurants.
5. We don't like shopping.
6. They likes time with Friend.
7. I like.
8. ______.

C. Classify the words in Exercise A.

Things usually outside	Things usually inside	Things inside or outside
books Computers		animals exercise family time games home work

D. **Read the information.**

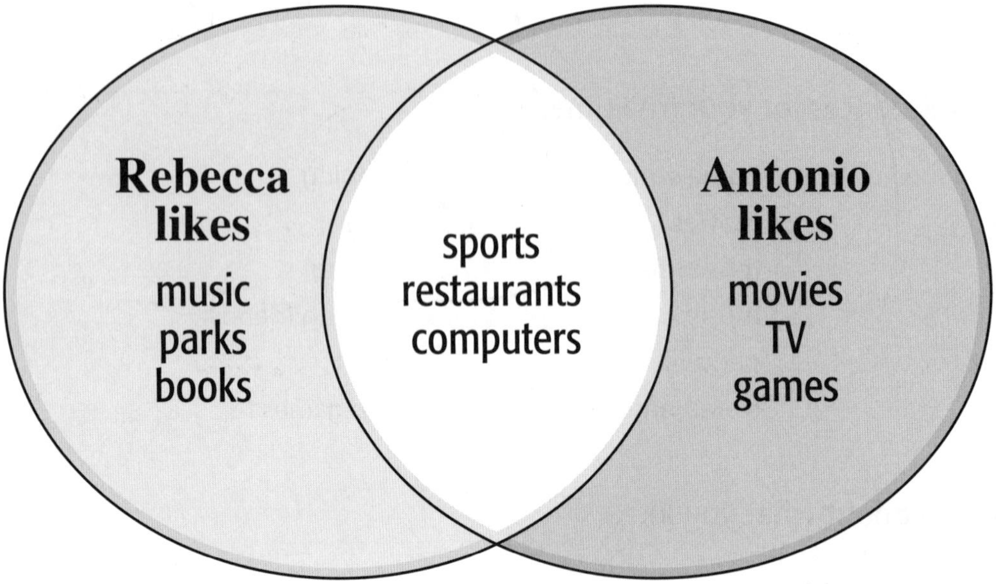

E. **Complete the chart.**

Only Rebecca likes . . .	Only Antonio likes . . .	Rebecca and Antonio like . . .
She likes the music	he likes movies	They like sports
She likes the parks	he likes TV	They like restaurants
She likes read books	he likes games	They like computers

F. **Read the chart.**

Simple Present: *Like*			
Subject	**Verb**	**Information**	**Example sentence**
I You We They	like	movies music sports games computers	I **like** movies. You **like** music. We **like** sports. They **like** games.
He She	likes		He **likes** games. She **likes** computers.

G. Circle the correct verb.

1. Amal **like** / **likes** computers.
2. They **like** / **likes** restaurants.
3. We **like** / **likes** school.
4. Maria and Alvin **like** / **likes** parks.
5. I **like** / **likes** books.
6. You **like** / **likes** the teacher.
7. I **like** / **likes** movies.
8. We **like** / **likes** sports.
9. Eva **like** / **likes** restaurants.
10. He **like** / **likes** music.
11. They **like** / **likes** TV.
12. She **like** / **likes** school.

H. Complete the paragraph with *like* and *likes*.

Allen is a teacher. Maria is Allen's wife. Allen likes computers. Maria ___likes___ restaurants. Maria and Allen ___like___ parks. Maria reads every day. She ___likes___ books. Allen listens to the radio every day. He ___likes___ music. They ___like___ sports, movies, and games. They are happy.

I. Complete the chart for Allen and Maria using the information in Exercise H.

Allen likes . . .	Maria likes . . .	Allen and Maria like . . .
likes ticher	likes wife	like parks
likes computers	likes restaurants	like sports
likes lisens radio	likes reads likes books	movies, games

J. Complete the chart for you and a partner.

I like . . .	My partner likes . . .	We like . . .
I like		

UNIT 1

LESSON 5 When do you study?

GOAL ■ Plan a schedule

A. Read the planner. Then, match the clocks to the activities.

Jim's Schedule

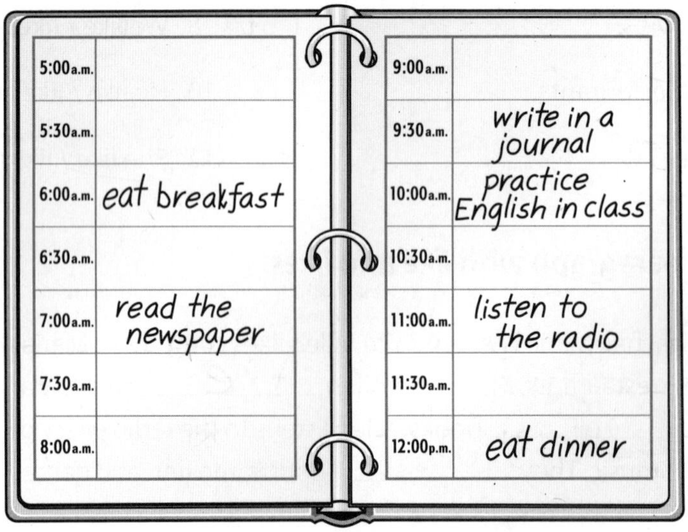

a. listen to the radio

b. practice English in class

c. read the newspaper

d. write in a journal

1.  c

2.  a

3.  d

4.  b

B. Write sentences about the schedule in Exercise A.

1. Jim eats breakfast at 6:00 a.m.
2. He reads the news paper at 7:00 a m.
3. He writes write in a journal at 9:30 a.m.
4. He practices English in class at 10:00 a.m.
5. He listens to the radio at 11:00 a.m.
6. He eats dinner eat dinner at 12:00 a.m.

C. Read the paragraphs. When do the people study? Mark the calendar.

My name is Mario. I want to learn English, so I need to study a lot. I will study a little bit on Mondays and a lot on Wednesdays. Wednesday is my day off from work so I have more time. I hope to watch TV in English on Saturdays, too.

My name is Sebastien. I'm from Haiti. I need to learn English so I can get a better job. I need to study Monday to Saturday. I want to take a break on Sunday to meet my friends and relax.

I'm Natalia. English is important. I need to study a lot. I think I will study every day for about two hours. I don't work so I have the time to study.

	Sunday	Monday	Tuesday	Wednesday	Thursday	Friday	Saturday
Mario		*x*		*x*			*x*
Sebastien	break	study	X	X	X	X	study
Natalia		study	study	study	study	study	study

D. Read the chart.

Using *from . . . to . . .*				
From	**Start time**	***To***	**End time**	**Example sentence**
from	7:00	to	8:00	He attends school **from** 7:00 **to** 8:00.
	10:30		11:00	He reads **from** 10:30 **to** 11:00.
	5:00		7:00	He practices English **from** 5:00 **to** 7:00.
	8:00		10:00	He watches TV **from** 8:00 **to** 10:00.

E. Rewrite the sentences with *from* and *to*.

1. Jerome reads.

   Jerome reads from 7:00 to 8:00.

2. Binh practices English.

   Binh practice from 5:00 to 7:00

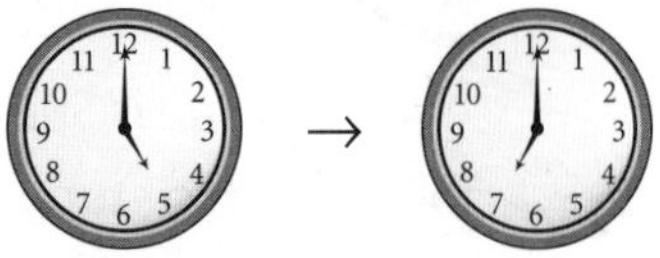

3. Alberto writes in a journal.

   Alberto writes From 9:30 to 10:00

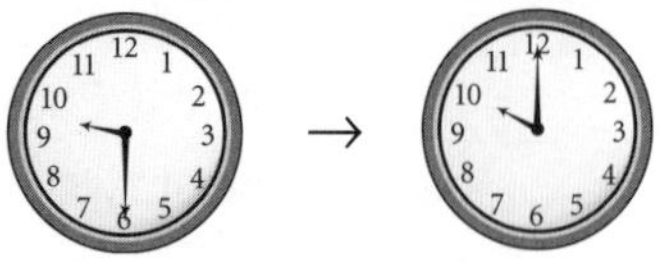

4. Marie listens to the radio.

   Marie listens to radio 12:00 to 12:10

5. Hugo watches TV.

   Hugo watches tv From 7:30 to 10:00

6. Tien reads the newspaper.

   Tien reads the newspaper from 7:00 to 7:30

F. Read the schedule and write sentences.

	Barry's Schedule		
	Start	End	Activity
1.	7:00 a.m.	7:15 a.m.	Barry eats breakfast.
2.	9:00 a.m.	10:30 a.m.	Barry practices English.
3.	10:30 a.m.	12:00 p.m.	Barry listens to the radio.

1. Barry eats from 7:00 a.m. to 7:15 a.m.
2. Barry practices English From 9:00 a.m to 10:30 a.m
3. Barry listens to the Radio from 10:30 a.m to 12: p.m

G. When do you do these things? Write the times.

1. I practice English ______.
2. I watch TV ______.
3. I listen to the radio ______.

UNIT 1

PRACTICE TEST

A. Read the questions. Circle the correct answers.

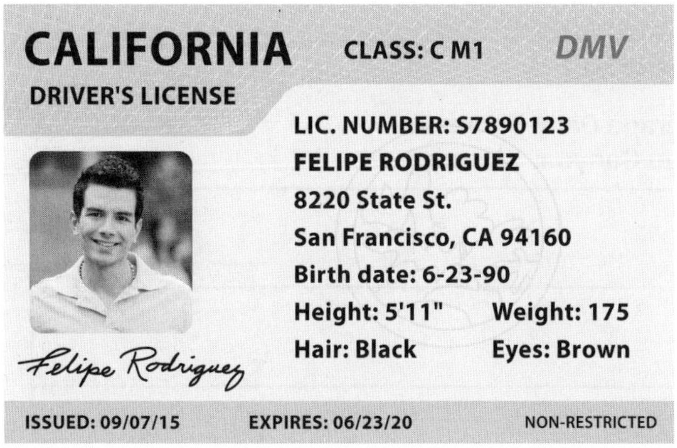

1. How tall is Felipe?
   a. 8220
   b. 175 pounds
   c. 5 feet 11 inches
   d. black hair

2. How much does Felipe weigh?
   a. 5′5″
   b. 175 pounds
   c. 6-23-85
   d. brown eyes

Jack's Schedule		
Start	**End**	**Activity**
7:00 a.m.	7:30 a.m.	eats breakfast
7:30 a.m.	8:30 a.m.	studies English
8:30 a.m.	9:00 a.m.	watches TV
9:00 a.m.	12:00 p.m.	learns in English class
12:00 p.m.	1:00 p.m.	eats lunch

3. When does Jack watch TV?
   a. at 8:30 a.m. to 9:00 a.m.
   b. to 8:30 a.m. from 9:00 a.m.
   c. from 8:30 a.m. to 9:00 a.m.
   d. 7:30 a.m. – 8:30 a.m.

4. When does Jack start breakfast?
   a. eats breakfast
   b. 7:00 a.m.
   c. 7:30
   d. studies English

UNIT 2

LESSON 1 Shopping

GOAL ■ Identify types of retail stores

A. Read the bar graph and answer the questions.

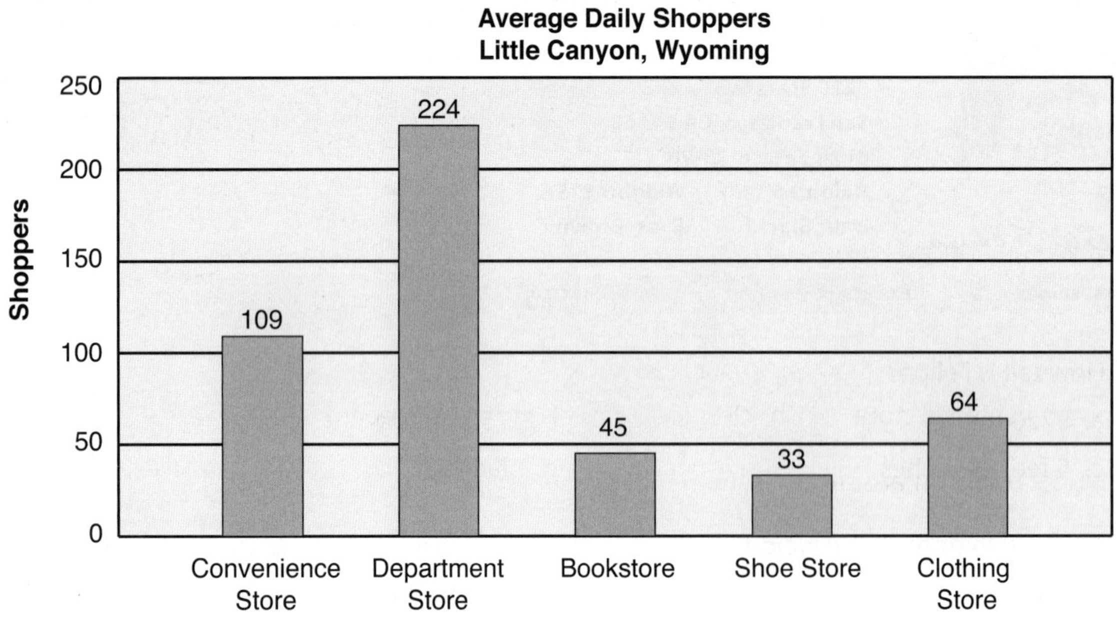

1. How many people shop at the bookstore? 45
2. How many people shop at the shoe store? ________
3. How many people shop at the convenience store? ________
4. How many people shop at the clothing store? ________
5. How many people shop at the department store? ________

B. Where do you shop more? Rank the list from 1–5. *1* is where you shop more.

_____ convenience store

_____ department store

_____ bookstore

_____ shoe store

_____ clothing store

C. Read the chart and circle the correct answers.

Name	Department store	Convenience store	Supermarket	Bookstore	Shoe store	Clothing store
Richard	shoes, pants	milk, water	groceries	dictionaries		shirts
Alexis	toys	oranges	groceries		shoes	shirts

1. Where do Alexis and Richard shop for groceries?
   a. convenience store b. supermarket c. department store
2. Where does Alexis shop for toys?
   a. bookstore b. convenience store c. department store
3. Where does Alexis shop for shirts?
   a. convenience store b. clothing store c. department store
4. Where does Richard shop for shoes?
   a. shoe store b. department store c. clothing store
5. Where does Richard shop for shirts?
   a. shoe store b. department store c. clothing store
6. Where does Alexis shop for oranges?
   a. convenience store b. supermarket c. department store
7. Where does Richard shop for pants?
   a. shoe store b. department store c. clothing store
8. What do Alexis and Richard shop for in the clothing store?
   a. pants b. shirts c. shoes

D. Read the chart.

Simple Present: *Shop*		
Subject	**Verb**	**Example sentence**
I, You, We, They	shop	I **shop** for shoes at a department store. You **shop** for bread at a convenience store. We **shop** for shorts at a department store. They **shop** for books at a bookstore.
He, She, It	shops	He **shops** for shoes at a shoe store. She **shops** for dresses at a clothing store.

E. Check (✓) the correct answers.

1. They ____________ for CD players at a department store.	☐ shop	☐ shops
2. We ____________ for books at the bookstore.	☐ shop	☐ shops
3. I ____________ for shirts at a clothing store.	☐ shop	☐ shops
4. Marcos and Renee ____________ for food at Sam's Supermarket.	☐ shop	☐ shops
5. Eva ____________ for a dress at Cool Breeze Clothing Store.	☐ shop	☐ shops
6. Van and her husband ____________ for shoes at a department store.	☐ shop	☐ shops
7. Armand ____________ for flowers at the flower shop.	☐ shop	☐ shops
8. Gabriela, Ana, and Paula ____________ for clothes every month.	☐ shop	☐ shops
9. You ____________ for toys at a toy store.	☐ shop	☐ shops
10. Lidia and I ____________ at Ruben's Food and Plenty.	☐ shop	☐ shops

F. Complete sentences using the information in Exercise C.

1. Richard shops for shoes and pants at the department store.
2. Alexis shop for toys? at the department store.
3. Richard and Alexis shop for grocerios? at the supermarket.
4. Alexis shop for shirts? at the clothing store.
5. Richard shop for shoes? at the bookstore.
6. Richard shop for shirts? at the convenience store.
7. Richard and Alexis Shirts at the clothing store.
8. Alexis shor for orange? at the department store.

G. Answer the questions about you.

1. Where do you shop for clothes? **Location:** ____________________
2. Where do you shop for milk? **Location:** ____________________
3. Where do you shop for a paper? **Location:** ____________________
4. Where do you shop for CDs? **Location:** ____________________

UNIT 2

LESSON 2 Van's purchases

GOAL ■ Make purchases and read receipts

A. Look at the advertisements and complete the chart.

T-shirt

dress shirt

dress

blue jeans

tennis shoes

shoes

Quantity	Unit price	Item	Total
Two pairs	$33.00	blu jeans	$66.00
Four	$ 16	T-shirt	$64.00
Three	$24.00	dress shirt	$72.00
Two pairs	$30.00	tennis shoes	$60.00
One	$54.00	dress	$54.00

B. Read the receipt and answer the questions.

MacKay's DEPARTMENT STORE	
Vacuum	$98.99
Washing machine	$450.00
Telephone	$80.00
Toaster	$42.99
Subtotal	$671.98
Tax	$53.76
TOTAL	**$725.74**

1. How much is the vacuum cleaner? $ 98:99
2. How much is the toaster? $ 42:99
3. How much is the telephone? $ 80.00
4. What's the tax? $ 53.76
5. What's the total? $ 725.74

C. Read the chart.

***Be* Verb (Questions)**			
Question words	***Be***	**Nouns**	**Sample questions**
how much (money)	is	the vacuum the radio	How much **is** the vacuum? How much **is** the radio?
how much (money)	are	the shoes the oranges	How much **are** the shoes? How much **are** the oranges?

D. Complete the sentences with *are* or *is*.

1. How much ___is___ the cheese?
2. How much ___are___ the oranges?
3. How much ___are___ the shirt?
4. How much ___is___ the sneakers?
5. How much ___are___ the hats?
6. How much ___is___ the book?
7. How much ___are___ the pencils?
8. How much ___is___ the pens?

E. Write questions with the information below.

1. (radio) How much is the radio?
2. (T-shirts) How much are the T-shirts ?
3. (dictionary) How much is the dictionary ?
4. (socks) How much are the socks ?
5. (shoes) How much are the shoes ?
6. (dress) How much is the dress ?
7. (bread) " " " " bread ?
8. (CD player) " " " " CD player. ?

F. Look at the pictures and complete the questions with *How much is* and *How much are*.

1. ______________________________ T-shirts?
2. ______________________________ the radio?
3. ______________________________ the dictionary?
4. ______________________________ socks?

G. Write items you want to buy. Look on the Internet or go to a store and find prices.

Item	Price
shoes	$18.00

UNIT 2

LESSON 3 Buying new clothes

GOAL ■ Identify articles of clothing

A. Read the conversations and complete the chart. Write an "x" under the clothes in the chart that are in the conversations.

	Shoes	Socks	Coat	Sweater	Dress
1.			*x*	*x*	
2.	X	X			
3.	X				X

1. **Salesperson:** Can I help you?
   Ben: Yes, I'm going on vacation and need some things.
   Salesperson: OK. Where are you going?
   Ben: I'm going to ski, but I don't have clothes for cold weather.
   Salesperson: Let's look at the coats and sweaters over here.
2. **Salesperson:** What can I do for you?
   Margaret: I need some shoes.
   Salesperson: Do you want formal shoes or something casual?
   Margaret: I need tennis shoes for walking in the park. What do you have?
   Salesperson: Here are some. You need socks too, right?
   Margaret: That's right.
3. **Salesperson:** Can I help you?
   Amy: Yes, I need a dress for a very important event.
   Salesperson: Our dresses are over here next to the women's shoe department.
   Amy: Thank you. I want to buy some shoes, too.
   Salesperson: Let me help you.
   Amy: Thanks.

B. Complete the sentences about Exercise A.

1. Ben needs a coat and sweater for cold weather.
2. Margaret needs shoes and socks for walking in the park.
3. Amy needs shoes Dress for an important event.

C. **Look at the receipt. Fill in the missing numbers.**

MacKay's DEPARTMENT STORE	
Baseball cap	$12.99
Blouse	$32.□9
Sweater	$4□.00
Suit	$2□5.4□
Tax	$25.□7
TOTAL	**$388.40**

each=cada

D. **Write the prices.**

baseball cap	blouse	sweater	suit
$ 12.99	$ ________	$ ________	$ ________

E. **Read the charts.**

***Be* Verb (Questions)**			
Question words	***Be***	**Nouns**	**Example question**
how much (money)	is	the dress	How much **is** the dress?
how much (money)	are	the socks	How much **are** the socks?

***Be* Verb (Answers)**		
Subject	***Be***	**Example sentence**
It (the dress, the suit, etc.)	is	It **is** $48. It**'s** $48. (the dress) It **is** $285. It**'s** $285. (the suit)
They (the socks, the ties, etc.)	are	They **are** $12. They**'re** $12. (the socks) They **are** $22. They**'re** $22. (the ties)

F. Check (✓) the correct answers.

1. (dress) it is $56.00. ☐ It is ☐ They are
2. (shoes) they are $28.00. ☐ It is ☐ They are
3. (skirt) it's $33.00. ☐ It's ☐ They're
4. (sweater) it is $34.99. ☐ It is ☐ They are
5. (ties) it is $12.99. ☐ It is ☐ They are
6. (tennis shoes) they are $22.50. ☐ It's ☐ They're
7. (hat) it's $24.00. ☐ It's ☐ They're
8. (T-shirts) it's $9.99. ☐ It's ☐ They're

G. Write three sentences. Follow the example.

1. shoes / $28.00
   The shoes are $28.00.
   They are $28.00.
   They're $28.00.
2. blouse / $45.00
3. suit / $385.98
4. socks / $15.45
5. tie / $25.55
6. coat / $75.99

H. Complete the receipt with information from Exercise F.

MacKay's DEPARTMENT STORE	
Shoes	$28.00
TOTAL	

UNIT 2

LESSON 4 What color is your shirt?

GOAL ■ Describe clothing

A. Read the conversations and complete the chart.

Conversation 1

Salesperson: Can I help you?

Omar: Yes, I need a few things.

Salesperson: OK. What's first?

Omar: I need a pair of black pants and a white shirt for work tomorrow.

Salesperson: Come right this way.

Conversation 2

Salesperson: What can I do for you?

Eddie: I can't find what I need. I think I'll go somewhere else.

Salesperson: Are you sure? What are you looking for?

Eddie: I'm looking for black shoes, very large shoes.

Salesperson: That's no problem. We have large shoes in the back.

Conversation 3

Terri: Excuse me. Where are clothes for children over 12?

Salesperson: They are in the junior section.

Terri: Over there?

Salesperson: Yes, over there. What exactly are you looking for?

Terri: I'm looking for a blue dress for my daughter and brown pants for my son.

Salesperson: You've come to the right place. Come this way.

Teri: Thank you.

Conversation 4

Salesperson: May I help you?

Marie: Yes. Can you direct me to the women's clothing?

Salesperson: The women's clothing is around the corner.

Marie: Thank you. I need a new outfit for a job interview.

Salesperson: So you want a dress or suit, right?

Marie: I want a blue dress and blue shoes.

Salesperson: I'm sure we can help you.

Marie: Thank you for your help.

	Color	Clothing
Omar		
Omar		
Eddie		
Terri's daughter		
Terri's son		
Marie		
Marie		

B. Read the descriptions and complete the sentences.

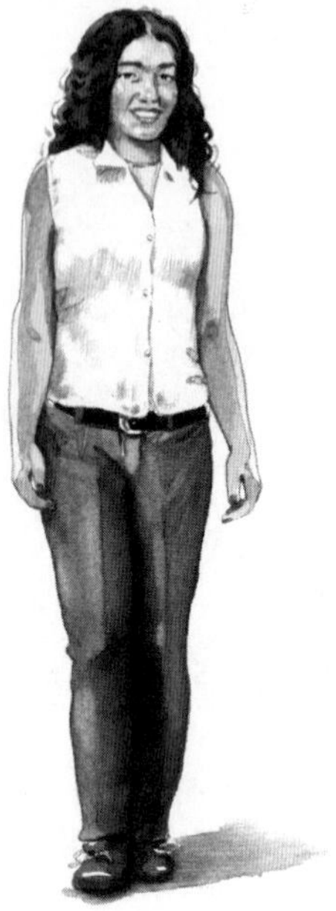

white blouse
blue pants
brown shoes
black belt

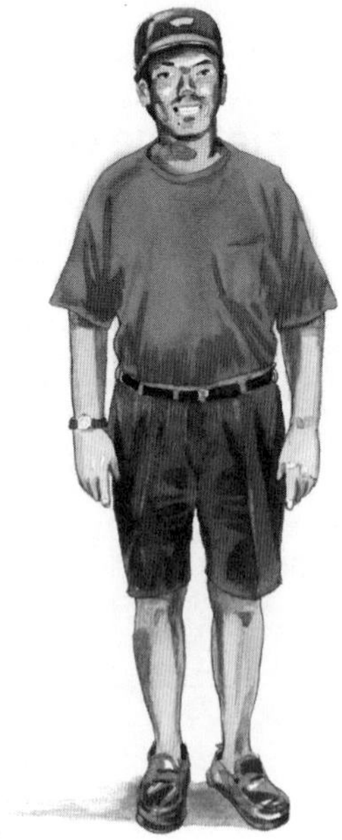

red shirt
brown shorts
brown sandals
blue cap

1. Gabriela has a ____________ blouse.
2. She has ____________ pants.
3. She has ____________ shoes.
4. She has a ____________ belt.
5. Roberto has a ____________ shirt.
6. He has ____________ shorts.
7. He has ____________ sandals.
8. He has a ____________ cap.

C. Read the chart.

Possessive Adjectives	
Possession	**Possessive adjectives**
I have a blue shirt.	**My** shirt is blue.
You have a green blouse.	**Your** blouse is green.
He has red shoes.	**His** shoes are red.
She has white pants.	**Her** pants are white.
We have blue hats.	**Our** hats are blue.
They have black shorts.	**Their** shorts are black.

D. Write the possessive adjective.

1. They have blue shirts. ___Their___ shirts are blue.
2. I have red shorts. ___My___ shorts are red.
3. We have black shoes. ___Our___ shoes are black.
4. You have a white blouse. ___youre___ blouse is white.
5. She has a green coat. ___her___ coat is green.
6. Anton and I have brown sandals. ___Our___ sandals are brown.
7. Elizabeth and Mario have black pants. ___theire___ pants are black.
8. I have a brown and a black belt. ___My___ belts are brown and black.

E. Write sentences about Oscar, Tom, and Catalina.

Oscar
red shirt
blue pants
black shoes
black belt

Tom
blue shirt
blue pants
black shoes
brown belt

Catalina
blue blouse
gray pants
black shoes
black belt

1. Oscar / shirt
   His shirt is red.
2. Tom / belt
   his brown belt
3. Catalina / pants
   her pants is gray
4. Oscar, Tom, and Catalina / shoes
   there shoes are blak
5. Oscar, Tom / pants
   There pants are blue
6. Catalina / blouse
   her blouse is blue

UNIT 2

LESSON 5 A large TV or a small TV?

GOAL ■ Describe items in a store

A. Read the paragraph and complete the chart.

My name is Barry. I live in the United States. I want many things. Some things are very important. I need the important things first.

I want a new house, but I need money first. I want a new car, but I need a used car right now. I need new clothes, I need a new job, and I need a new computer. I want a new $2,000 computer, but I only need a $1,000 computer. It is difficult to know what I need right now and what I want.

B. Complete the chart with what Barry wants and needs.

He needs . . .	He wants . . .
money	new house
He needs used Car	new car
	2,000.00 computer
clothes	
1,000.00 — computer	

C. Write sentences with the information in the chart from Exercise B.

1. Barry needs money.
2. He needs a used car.
3. He needs 1,000 - Computer. .
4. He needs new clothes.
5. He needs things first. .
6. He wants a new house.
7. He wants new Car.
8. He wants 2,000 - Computer. .

D. Match the adjective with the picture. Draw a line.

small

old

medium

striped

E. Using the information in Exercise D, complete the following sentences.

1. He wants a small computer and not a ___big___ computer.
2. He wants an old car and not a ___New___ car.
3. She wants a medium blouse and not a ___large___ blouse.
4. He wants a striped shirt and not a ___Plaid___ shirt.

F. Read the chart.

Adjectives				
Subject	**Verb**	**Adjective**	**Noun**	**Example sentence**
I You We They	want	a big a large a little a small an old a new a used a medium	TV book house blouse car shirt	I want a **big** TV. You want a **small** house. We want an **old** book. They want a **used** car.
He She	wants			He wants a **big** shirt. She wants a **medium** blouse. *Note:* Use *a* or *an* with singular count nouns.

G. Check (✓) the correct answers.

1. I ___want___ a new car.	☐ want	☐ wants
2. The teacher ___wants___ a small radio.	☐ want	☐ wants
3. The students ___Wants___ a large TV in the classroom.	☐ want	☐ wants
4. We ___wants___ an old car.	☐ want	☐ wants
5. You ___want___ a small apartment.	☐ want	☐ wants
6. They ___wants___ an old book from the library.	☐ want	☐ wants
7. I ___want___ a little dog.	☐ want	☐ wants
8. He ___want___ a large T-shirt.	☐ want	☐ wants

H. Read the descriptions of what Nam, Silvia and Roberto, and Gabriela want. Write sentences about them. – a ellos

Nam
new house
used car

Silvia and Roberto
old house
new car

Gabriela
old house
used car

1. Nam wants a new house and a used car.
2. Silvia and Roberto they want a old house and anew car.
3. Gabriela She want a old house andaused car.
4. Nam and Gabriela they want anew house and a old house.
5. Silvia, Roberto, and Gabriela they want a old house, and a used car.

PRACTICE TEST

A. Look at the ads and receipts. Read the questions. Circle the correct answers.

Martin's Department Store

Date: 09-06-2015

Shirt .... 2@$17.98 -	$35.96
Shoes	$22.99
Subtotal	$58.95
Tax	$4.72
TOTAL	$63.67

Customer Copy

HERO BOOKS

Date: 09-06-2015

Bilingual dictionary	$21.95
Subtotal	$21.95
Tax	$1.76
TOTAL	$23.71

No Returns Without Receipt

Sam's Food Mart

Date: 09-06-2015

Bread	$2.30
Cheese	$2. 75
Oranges @.99 a pound	$1.98
Potato Chips	$2. 60
TOTAL	$9.63

THANK YOU for shopping at Sam's.

1. How much is one shirt?
   a. $35.96
   b. Martin's Department Store
   c. Total
   d. $17.98

2. What is the price of a dictionary before tax?
   a. $1.76
   b. $21.95
   c. $23.71
   d. free

3. How much are the sneakers?
   a. $17
   b. $285
   c. $33
   d. $84

4. How much is the sweater?
   a. $12
   b. $35
   c. $36
   d. $84

UNIT 3

LESSON 1 What's for lunch?

GOAL ■ Identify common meals and foods

A. Make a list of food you like for each meal.

Breakfast	Lunch	Dinner
*cheese * beans * Sausage * ham	- chicken - beef - water - beans	- pizza - Rice - beans

I like . . .	I don't like . . .
1) I like cheese, and beans for	
Breakfast	
2) I like for lunch, chicken	
and Rice	
3) I like to eat for dinner Rice, beans	

B. Make a list of food you don't like for each meal.

Breakfast	Lunch	Dinner

C. Write sentences about your lists.

1. I like ______________ for breakfast.
2. I like ______________ for breakfast.
3. I like ______________ for breakfast.
4. I like ______________ for lunch.
5. I like ______________ for lunch.
6. I like ______________ for lunch.
7. I like ______________ for dinner.
8. I like ______________ for dinner.
9. I like ______________ for dinner.
10. I don't like ______________ for breakfast.
11. I don't like ______________ for breakfast.
12. I don't like ______________ for breakfast.
13. I don't like ______________ for lunch.
14. I don't like ______________ for lunch.
15. I don't like ______________ for lunch.
16. I don't like ______________ for dinner.
17. I don't like ______________ for dinner.
18. I don't like ______________ for dinner.

D. Write what you like and what you don't like in the chart. Use the words from the box.

pizza	hamburger	eggs
fried chicken	turkey sandwich	cereal
chicken and rice	spaghetti	roast beef

I like . . .	I don't like . . .
I like pizza	I don't like hamburger
I like eggs	I " " Cereal
I like fried chicken	
I like chicken and rice	
I like turkey sandwich	
I like spaghetti	

E. Read the charts.

Simple Present: *Like*		
Subject	**Verb**	**Example sentence**
I, You, We, They	like	I **like** hamburgers. You **like** french fries. We **like** fried chicken. They **like** roast beef.
He, She, It	likes	He **likes** cereal. She **likes** toast.

Negative Simple Present: *Like*				
Subject	**Negative**	**Verb**	**Noun**	**Example sentence**
I, You, We, They	don't	like	hamburgers french fries fried chicken cereal	I **don't** like hamburgers. You **don't** like french fries.
He, She	doesn't			He **doesn't** like fried chicken. She **doesn't** like cereal.

F. Check (✓) the correct words.

1. Dave ______ pizza.	☐ don't like	☐ like	☑ doesn't like
2. Martha ______ roast beef.	☑ likes	☐ don't like	☐ like
3. Dave and Jane ______ cereal.	☑ like	☐ don't likes	☐ doesn't like
4. Ana ______ spaghetti.	☑ doesn't like	☐ like	☐ no like
5. We ______ fried chicken.	☑ like	☐ likes	☐ doesn't like
6. I ______ french fries.	☑ don't like	☐ likes	☐ no like
7. He ______ eggs and toast.	☐ like	☐ don't like	☑ doesn't like
8. You ______ peanut butter.	☑ like	☐ likes	☐ doesn't like

G. Complete the sentences about what Martha and Dave *like* and *don't like*.

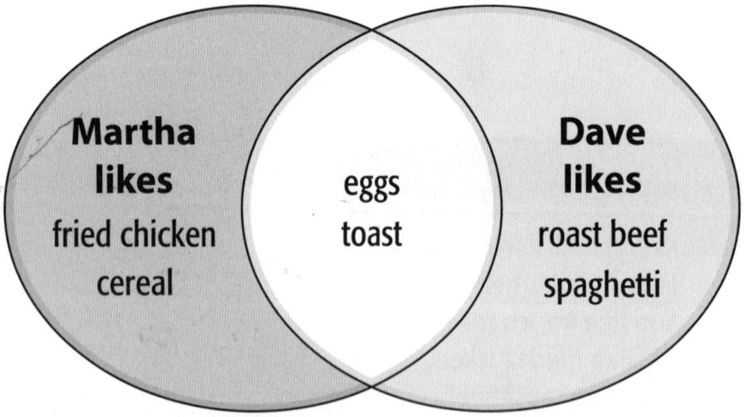

1. Martha likes eggs and fried chicken.
2. Dave and Martha likes eggs.
3. Martha doesn't like roast beef.
4. Dave and Martha likes toast.
5. Dave doesn't like fried chicken.
6. Dave and Martha likes eggs.

H. Write sentences about what you and a partner like.

1. I like roast beef.
2. My partner He likes roast beef.
3. We like pizza.

UNIT 3

LESSON 2 It's in the newspaper.

GOAL ■ Interpret food advertisements

A. Look at the advertisement and complete the chart.

Product	Container or quantity (jar, box, bag, pound, package, six-pack, gallon, each, or loaf)	Price
Peanut butter	a jar	$3.25
Spaghetti	package	$ 1.98
carrots	one-pound bag	1.25
tomatoes	pound	$.60
ground Beef	a Pound	$3.40
soda	six-pack	$2.99
milk	a gallon	$3.20
avocados	each	$.90

B. Look at the containers and complete the sentences with the information.

Quantity	Item	Container
2	milk	gallon
1	spaghetti	package
1	peanut butter	jar
3	soda	six-pack
3	cookies	box
3	potato chips	bag

1. There are two gallons of milk.
2. There is One Package of spaghetti.
3. There is One Jar of peanut butter.
4. There are thee six-pack of soda.
5. There are thee box of cookies.
6. There are thee bag of potato chips.

C. Read the charts.

How much / How many		
	Question	Answer
Noncount	**How much** milk is there?	There is one gallon of milk. There are two gallons of milk. There are three avocados.
Count	**How many** gallons of milk are there? **How many** avocados are there?	

Question words	Verb	Nouns	Example question
How much (money)	is	the milk	How much **is** the milk?
How much (money)	are	the tomatoes	How much **are** the tomatoes?

D. Write *How many* or *How much*.

1. How many gallons of milk are there?
2. How nany jars of mustard are there?
3. How much yogurt is there?
4. How many bags of potato chips are there?
5. How much is the spaghetti?
6. How many avocados are there?
7. How many packages of spaghetti are there?
8. How much are the tomatoes?
9. How much ground beef is there?
10. How much water is there?

E. Write *How much is* or *How much are*.

1. How much are the avocados?
2. How much the butter?
3. How much are the oranges?
4. How many the carrots?
5. How much are the ground beef?
6. How much the milk?
7. How many the sugar?
8. How much the cookies?

F. **Fill in the chart about what is in your home right now.**

Inventory		
Quantity	**Item**	**Container**
	milk	gallon
	spaghetti	package
	peanut butter	jar
	soda	six-pack
	cookies	box
	potato chips	bag

G. **Make a shopping list of things you need for the week. Write the prices.**

Item	Quantity	Price

UNIT 3

LESSON 3 What do we need?

GOAL ■ Express needs

A. Read the paragraph and complete the shopping list.

Vincent needs some food at the store. He makes a shopping list with everything he needs. For example, he needs one loaf of bread. He also need five pounds of ground beef. He needs three cans of tomato sauce and one package of spaghetti. He also wants an onion and some other spices. What do you think he plans to make?

	Shopping List
1)	Loaf of bread.
2)	ground beef.
3)	Tomato sauce.
4)	One package spaghetti
5)	Onion. other spice
	spices

B. Look at the shopping list and complete the conversations.

	Shopping List
	3 jars of peanut butter
	2 cans of soup
	2 bottles of oil
	3 packages of spaghetti
	3 cans of tomato sauce

Soup

Roberto: What do we need at the store?

Eva: We need ___soup___.

Roberto: How much do we need?

Eva: We need ___two cans___.

Tomato sauce

Roberto: What do we need at the store?

Eva: We need ___tomato sauce___.

Roberto: How much do we need?

Eva: We need ___three Cans___.

Spaghetti

Roberto: What do we need at the store?

Eva: We need ___Spaghetti___.

Roberto: How much do we need?

Eva: We need ___three Packages___.

Oil

Roberto: What do we need at the store?

Eva: We need ___Oil___.

Roberto: How much do we need?

Eva: We need ___two bottles___.

C. Read the chart.

Simple Present		
Subject	**Verb**	**Example sentence**
I, You, We, They	eat like need want make	I **eat** tacos for lunch. You **like** eggs for breakfast. We **need** three cans of corn. They **want** three boxes of cookies. I **make** sandwiches for lunch.
He, She, It	eats likes needs wants makes	He **eats** pizza for dinner. She **likes** tomato soup. He **needs** three pounds of tomatoes. She **wants** two bottles of water. She **makes** sandwiches for Duong.

D. Write the correct form of the verbs.

1. She ____eats____ (eat) roast beef sandwiches.
2. They ____Like____ (like) a big breakfast.
3. We ____Need____ (need) two gallons of water.
4. Vinicio and Laura ____want____ (want) tuna fish sandwiches.
5. I ____make____ (make) a turkey sandwich every day for lunch.
6. The students ____eat____ (eat) pizza every week.
7. He ____Likes____ (like) tomatoes on his hamburger.
8. Hugo and I ____Need____ (need) water and soda.
9. Pablo ____eats____ (eat) lunch at noon.
10. Minh ____Makes____ (make) sandwiches for Duong.

E. Look at the charts.

Duong			
Sandwiches	like	eat	make
turkey	X	X	
tuna fish		X	
roast beef	X	X	
peanut butter	X	X	X

Minh			
Sandwiches	like	eat	make
turkey	X	X	X
tuna fish	X	X	X
roast beef	X		
peanut butter			X

F. Complete the sentences with the correct form of the verbs. Look at Exercise E.

1. Minh ____makes____ turkey, tuna fish, and peanut butter sandwiches.
2. Duong doesn't like tuna fish, but he ____eats____ tuna fish.
3. Duong ____eats____ turkey, tuna fish, roast beef, and peanut butter sandwiches.
4. Duong and Minh ____eat____ tuna fish sandwiches.
5. Minh ____likes____ roast beef sandwiches.
6. Duong and Minh ____like____ roast beef sandwiches.

UNIT 3

LESSON 4 What's cheaper?

GOAL ■ Compare prices

A. Read the sign over the highway fruit stand.

B. Answer the questions with the information in Exercise A.

1. Bita bought 2 pounds of apples. She spent __$4__.
2. Miyuki bought a dozen limes. She spent __$3__.
3. Juan bought a dozen lemons. He spent __$4__.
4. Charity bought a pound of bananas, a papaya, and a mango. She spent __$3.25__.
5. Morteza bought a pound of grapes and a pound of bananas. He spent __$2__.
6. Lam bought 10 oranges. They weighed 1½ pounds. He spent __$4.50__.
7. Hilda bought 3 pounds of tomatoes. She spent __$3.75__.
8. Lilia bought a papaya and Courtney bought a mango. They spent __2.75__.

C. Read the chart.

Food	Van's Supermarket	Albert's Supermarket
bananas	$1.25 a pound	$1.35 a pound
oil	$3.00 a bottle	$2.75 a bottle
tuna	$ .99 a can	$ .96 a can
cereal	$3.69 a box	$3.99 a box
jelly	$2.10 a jar	$2.25 a jar

D. Answer the questions with the information in Exercise C.

1. How much are the bananas at Albert's? $1.35 a pound
2. How much is the jelly at Van's? $2.10 jar
3. How much is one box of cereal plus one can of tuna at Van's? $3.69 box $.99 a can
4. How much is a bottle of oil plus a pound of bananas at Albert's? $1.35 a pound 2.75 bottle
5. How much is one bottle of oil plus a pound of bananas at Van's? 1.25 3. a bottle
6. How much is a jar of jelly at Albert's? $2.25 a jar

E. Read the chart.

Comparative Adjectives		
	Question	**Answer**
Singular	Where is ground beef cheaper?	It's cheaper at Puente Market.
Plural	Where are carrots cheaper?	They're cheaper at Food City.
	Question	**Answer**
Singular	Where is ground beef more expensive?	It's more expensive at Puente Market.
Plural	Where are carrots more expensive?	They're more expensive at Food City.

F. Look at Exercise C. Complete the sentences with *cheaper* or *more expensive*.

1. Bananas are ___cheaper___ at Van's.
2. Oil is ___cheaper___ at Albert's.
3. Cereal is ___more expensive___ at Albert's.
4. Tuna is ___cheaper___ at Albert's.
5. Jelly is ___more expensive___ at Albert's.
6. Oil is ___more expensive.___ at Van's.

G. Look at Exercise C. Write the name of the store.

1. Jelly is cheaper at ___Van's Supermarket___.
2. Tuna is more expensive at ___Van's Supermarket___.
3. Bananas are more expensive at ___Albert's Supermarket___.
4. Oil is cheaper at ___Albert's Supermarket.___.
5. Cereal is cheaper at ___Van's Supermarket.___.
6. Bananas are cheaper at ___Van's Supermarket.___.

H. Answer the questions with complete sentences.

1. Where are bananas cheaper?
   They're cheaper at Van's.
2. Where is tuna more expensive?
   They're more expensive at Van's supermarket
3. Where is oil cheaper?
   Albert's Supermarket
4. Where is cereal more expensive?
   Albert's Supermarket.
5. Where is jelly cheaper?
   Van's Supermarket.

I. Write prices from your store.

My Store

apples: $________

sugar: $________

carrots: $________

UNIT 3

LESSON 5 Buying lunch

GOAL ■ Take and place orders

A. Complete the menu with food from the box.

MARIO'S *Sandwich Shop*

SALADS	
fresh green salad	1.85
chicken salad	2.75
Caesar Salad	

BEVERAGES	
Coffee	1.00
soda	2.00
Milk	1.25

SANDWICHES	
Roast beef	2.75
Turkey	2.50
chicken	2.75
cheese	2.75

SIDE ORDERS	
potatoes chips	.89

Potato chips $.89	Turkey $2.50
Coffee $1.00	French fries $1.19
Roast beef $2.75	Soda $2.00
Tuna $2.50	Ham $2.50
Fresh green salad $1.85	Chicken salad $2.75
Milk $1.25	Caesar salad $2.75
	Cheese $2.25

B. Read the order.

Order

TABLE NO. 4	SERVER NO. Marilyn
1 roast beef sandwich	$ 3.99
1 order of french fries	$ 1.49
1 soda	$ .99
1 ice cream	$ 1.29
Tax	$ .54
TOTAL	$ 8.30

C. Answer the questions about the order in Exercise B with short answers.

1. How much is the tax? It's 54 cents.
2. How much is the total? It's 8.30
3. How much is the drink? it's .99
4. How much is the sandwich? it's 3.99
5. Does he want ice cream? yes
6. Does he want milk? Don't

D. Read the chart.

Short Answers		
Question	**Yes**	**No**
Do you want a hamburger?	Yes, I do.	No, I don't. Thank you.
Do they want sandwiches?	Yes, they do.	No, they don't.
Does he want a sandwich?	Yes, he does.	No, he doesn't.
Does she want a sandwich?	Yes, she does.	No, she doesn't.

E. Look at the chart and complete the questions

Name	Turkey sandwich	Soda	French fries	Chocolate ice cream
Sebastien	yes	yes	yes	yes
Ana	no	no	no	yes
Andre	yes	no	no	no
Kim	yes	no	yes	yes

1. Does Ana want ice cream? Yes, she does.
2. Does Andre want a soda? NO, he doesn't
3. Do Andre and Ana want french fries? No, they don't
4. Does Sebastien want a sandwich and french fries? yes, he does
5. Does Kim want a soda? No, She doesn't
6. Does Kim want a sandwich? Yes, she does.
7. Do Sebastien and Kim want ice cream? yes, they do
8. Does Ana want a sandwich? No, She doesint

F. Read the chart and complete the conversations.

	Turkey sandwich	Soda	French fries	Chocolate ice cream
Number 1	yes	yes	no	yes
Number 2	yes	no	yes	yes
Number 3	no	yes	yes	yes
Number 4	yes	yes	yes	no

Number 1

Server: Can I take your order?
Customer: *Yes. I want a turkey sandwich and a soda.*
Server: Do you want french fries?
Customer: *No, I don't.* Thank you.
Server: Do you want dessert?
Customer: *Yes, I do. I want chocolate ice cream.*
Server: OK.

Number 2

Server: Can I take your order?
Customer: yes I want a turkey sandwich and soda.
Server: Do you want french fries?
Customer: yes I do Thank you.
Server: Do you want dessert?
Customer: yes I do. I want chocolate ice
Server: OK.

Number 3

Server: Can I take your order?
Customer: No I don't
Server: Do you want french fries?
Customer: yes, I do Thank you.
Server: Do you want dessert?
Customer: yes I do. I wont chocolate ice
Server: OK.

Number 4

Server: Can I take your order?
Customer: yes, I want a turkey and a soda.
Server: Do you want french fries?
Customer: yes Thank you.
Server: Do you want dessert?
Customer: No, I don't
Server: OK.

PRACTICE TEST

A. Read the text and circle the correct answers.

John goes shopping every week. He buys many things that he needs for his lunches. He likes salad for lunch. He buys lettuce, apples, and carrots every week. Sometimes John shops at A-1 Market and sometimes he shops at Puente Market. Apples are cheaper at Puente Market. They are only $.99 cents a pound. Lettuce and carrots are more expensive. He shops at Puente Market because he likes the apples there.

1. Where does John shop?
   a. Puente Market b. apples
   c. carrots d. A-1 Market

2. How much are the apples at Puente Market?
   a. apples b. $.99
   c. lunch d. cheaper

John's Order	Allison's Order	Lien's Order
Cheeseburger	French Fries	Hot Dog
Milk	Ham Sandwich	Green Salad
Fruit Cup	Soda	Water

3. What is John's beverage?
   a. cheeseburger b. milk
   c. soda d. fruit cup

4. What is Alison's side order?
   a. french fries b. soda
   c. ham sandwich d. milk

5. What does Lien drink?
   a. hot dog b. water
   c. green salad d. milk

LESSON 1 A house or an apartment?

GOAL ■ Identify types of housing

A. Read about Rosa and Gilberto. Then put the sentences and questions in the correct column in the table.

I live in a condominium
It's on Adams Street.
I like my home.

I live in an apartment.
It's on Butcher Street.
I don't like my home. I want to move.

I live around the corner on Adams Street.

I live on Butcher Street. How about you?

I really like my home. It's perfect for me.

No. My home is a condominium.

Really. Do you live in a house?

That's nice. I don't like my home. I want to move.

~~Where do you live, Gilberto?~~

Rosa asks and answers	Gilberto asks and answers
Where do you live, Gilberto?	

B. Create a conversation with the sentences from the table.

Rosa: ______________________________

Gilberto: ______________________________

Rosa: ______________________________

Gilberto: ______________________________

Rosa: ______________________________

Gilberto: ______________________________

Rosa: ______________________________

Gilberto: ______________________________

C. Match the location with the problem. Draw a line.

1. 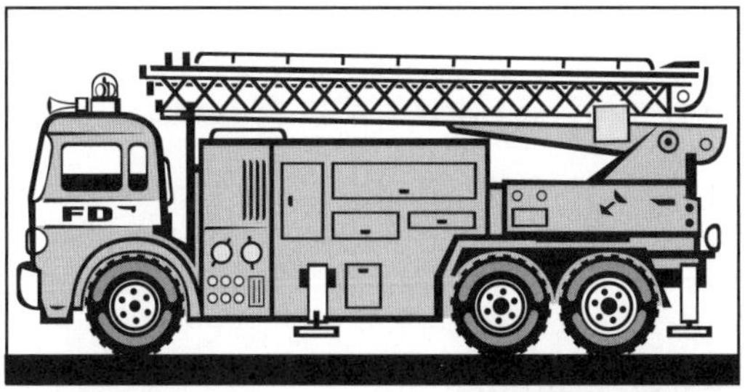

2. 

3. 

4. 

a. I need to learn English.

b. I need to send a package.

c. There is an emergency.

d. I need to relax.

D. Read the chart.

Need to			
Subject	***Need***	**Infinitive**	**Example sentence**
I, You, We, They	need	to go to drive to send to see to buy to look for	I **need to go** to the hospital. You **need to drive** to the store. We **need to send** a letter. They **need to see** the doctor.
He, She, It	needs		He **needs to buy** a book. She **needs to look for** a house.

E. Circle *need* or *needs*.

1. Ruby **need / needs** to work in the factory on Friday to pay the rent.
2. They **need / needs** to go to the real estate agent to find a house.
3. Antonio **need / needs** to visit the DMV to get a license.
4. We **need / needs** to find a hotel to sleep tonight.
5. I **need / needs** to go to the dentist's office to have an examination.
6. She **need / needs** to go to school to learn English.

F. Look at the sentences in Exercise E. Answer the questions.

1. Why does Ruby need to work? To pay the rent.
2. Why do they need to go to the real estate office? ______
3. Why does Antonio need to visit the DMV? ______
4. Why do we need to find a hotel? ______
5. Why do you need to go to the dentist? ______
6. Why does she need to go to school? ______

G. Use *need* or *needs* and the words in the box to complete the sentences.

~~go to the hospital~~	drive to the park	send a letter	see a police officer
buy a new car	look for a new house	talk to the doctor	eat lunch

1. She is very sick. She needs to go to the hospital.
2. They live in an apartment. They ______.
3. Marco is at the post office. He ______.
4. He has a driver's license but no car. He ______.
5. We are hungry. Let's find a good restaurant. We ______.
6. You are going to Doctor Smith's office. You ______.
7. You lost your purse. You ______.
8. The park is five miles from here. I ______.

UNIT 5

LESSON 2 Where is City Hall?

GOAL ■ Give and follow directions

A. Study the map.

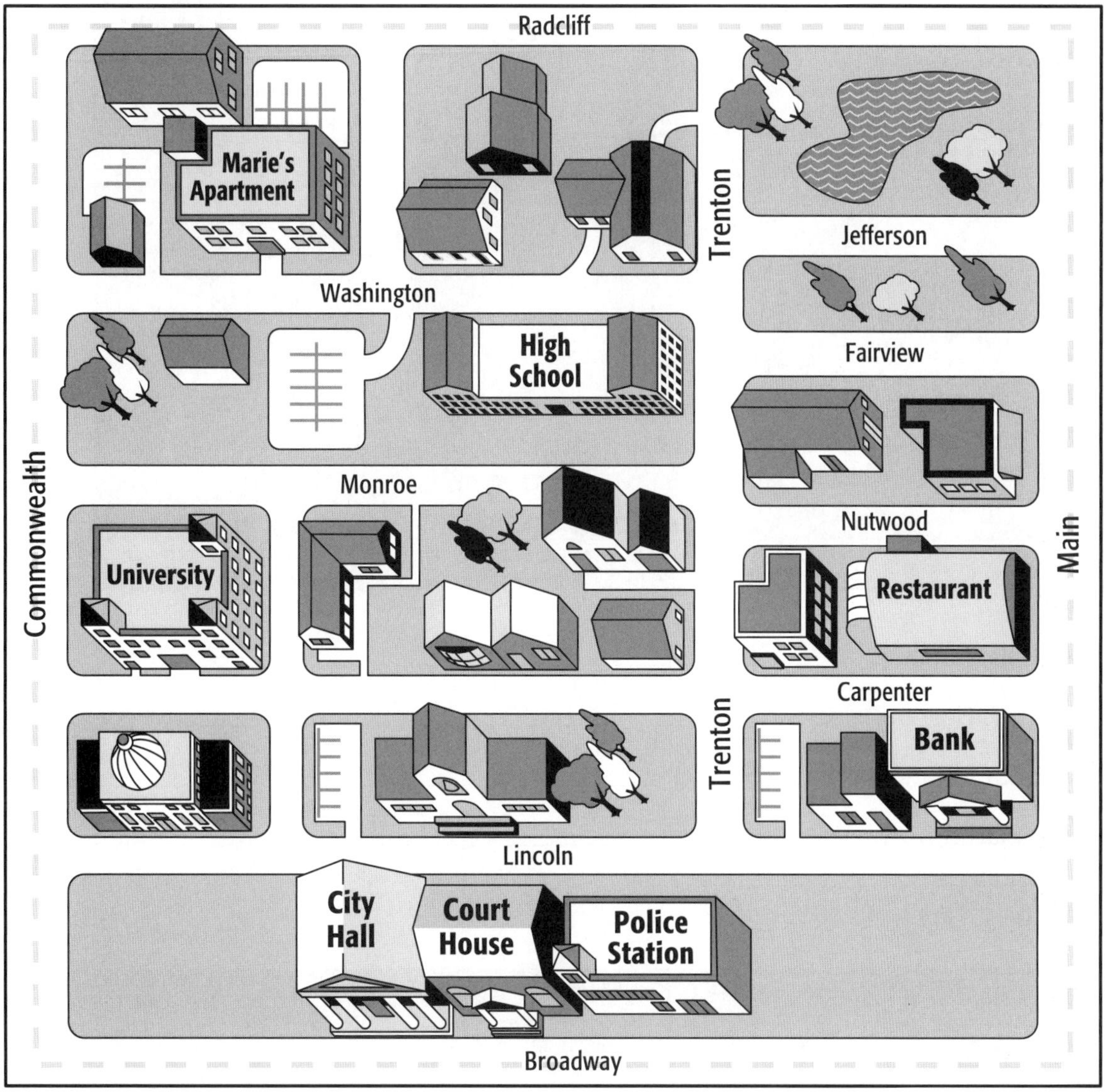

B. Write sentences about the map.

1. ______________________ is around the corner from ______________________.
2. __________________ is between __________________ and __________________.
3. ____________________________ is next to ____________________________.
4. ____________________________ is across from ____________________________.

C. Look at the map and complete the sentences.

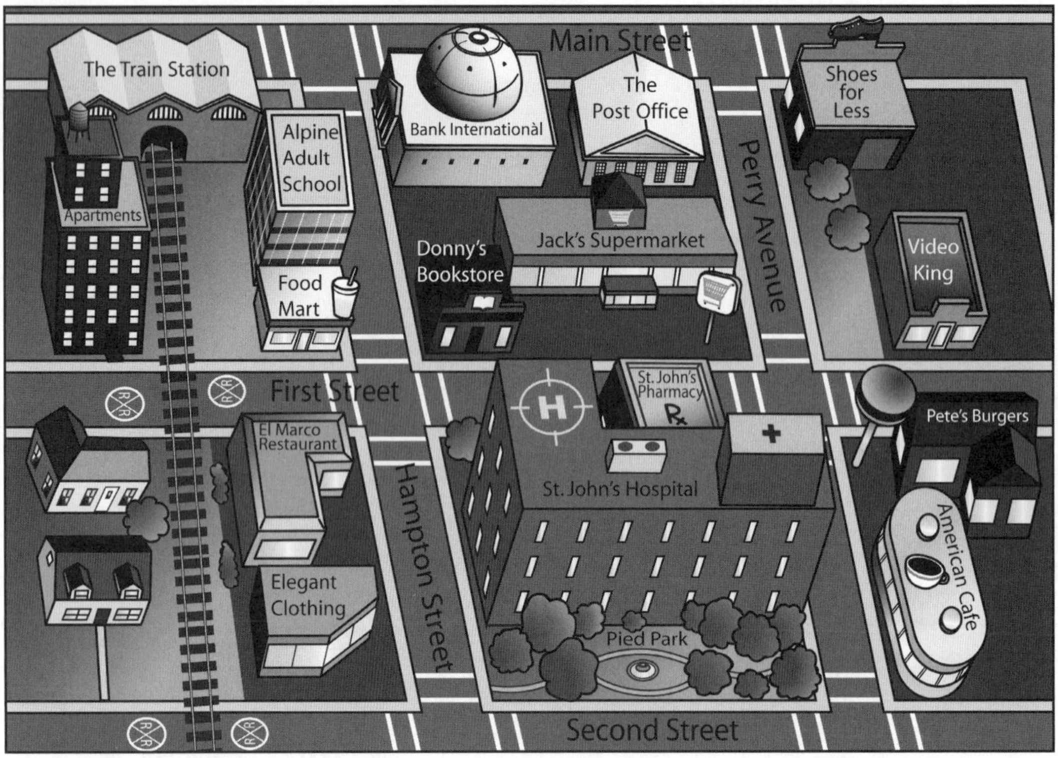

1. The train station is on ______Main______ Street.
2. St. John's Hospital is on ____________ Street.
3. Elegant Clothing is on the corner of ____________ and ____________.
4. Food Mart is on ____________ Street.

D. Read the chart.

Imperatives			
Subject	**Verb**		**Example sentence**
You	turn	left	**Turn** left.
You	turn	right	**Turn** right.
You	turn	around	**Turn** around.
You	go	straight ahead	**Go** straight ahead.
You	stop		**Stop!**
You	make	a U-turn	**Make** a U-turn.
Example: Go straight ahead. Turn left at First Street. Turn right on Main Street. Stop.			

E. Check (✓) the correct verb in the imperative.

1. ______ left on First Street.	☐ Turns	☑ Turn	☐ He turns
2. ______ on the left.	☐ Stop	☐ Stops	☐ Is stopping
3. ______ straight ahead.	☐ Going	☐ goes	☐ Go
4. ______ around.	☐ Stop	☐ Turns	☐ Turn
5. ______ right at the intersection.	☐ Is turning	☐ Going	☐ Turn
6. ______!	☐ Goes	☐ Turning	☐ Stop

F. Add periods and capital letters to the directions.

1. turn around go straight ahead three miles turn left on Mulberry Avenue turn right on Prentice Street stop on the left

   Turn around. Go straight ahead three miles. Turn left on Mulberry Avenue. Turn right on Prentice Street. Stop on the left.

2. go straight ahead to Montgomery Street turn left on Main stop on the left

   ____

   ____

3. turn left on Fifth Avenue turn right on Kennedy Street stop straight ahead

   ____

   ____

4. make a U-turn turn on Adams go straight ahead three blocks stop on the right

   ____

   ____

5. turn right on Jacob's Place make a U-turn at the light turn left on Pine stop

   ____

   ____

G. Write directions from your school to your home.

____

____

____

____

LESSON 3 Let's go to the mall!

GOAL ■ Give and follow directions in a mall

A. Scan the directory and complete the questions with names of stores. Write all the stores you can name.

LANDSBURY MALL DIRECTORY

Cosmetics
Hair and Nails **A-1**
Fashion Stylists **C-6**

Jewelry
Ziggy's **B-5**

Optical and Eyewear
Don's Optometry **B-7**
Landsbury Shades **C-9**

Shoes
Shoe Emporium **A-2**
Sport Runner **B-11**
Walk A Lot **B-12**

Department Stores
Reed's **B-14**
Torkelson's **B-1**

Men's Apparel
Tall Man **B-6**
Ryan's Suit and Tie **C-3**

Pets
The Pet Club **C-5**

Toys
Darla's Toys C-4
The Toy Rack **B-4**

Gifts
Mostly Gifts **B-3**
Shaffers **B-13**
The Real Thing **C-1**

Restaurants and Specialty Foods
Bloomfield's Steakhouse **B-2**
Ice Cream Heaven **B-10**
Jay's Hamburgers **C-2**
Marina's Coffee Café **C-7**
The Chocolate Factory **C-8**

Women's Apparel
Dresses and More B-9
The Casual Woman B-9

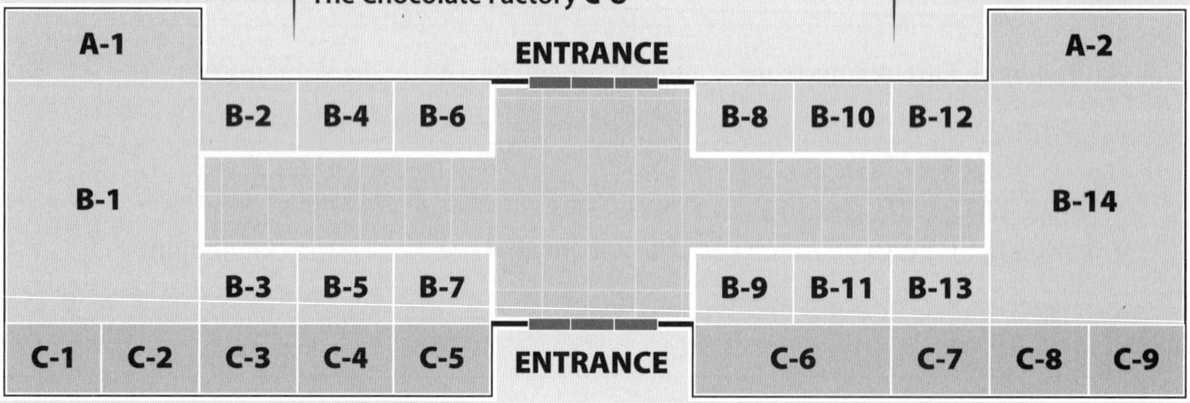

1. I need a haircut. Where can I go? Hair and Nails, Fashion Stylist
2. I want a cat. Where can I go? ____________
3. I want a big hamburger. Where can I go? ____________
4. I need a gift for a friend. Where can I go? ____________
5. I need my eyes checked. Where can I go? ____________

B. Look at the map and answer the questions

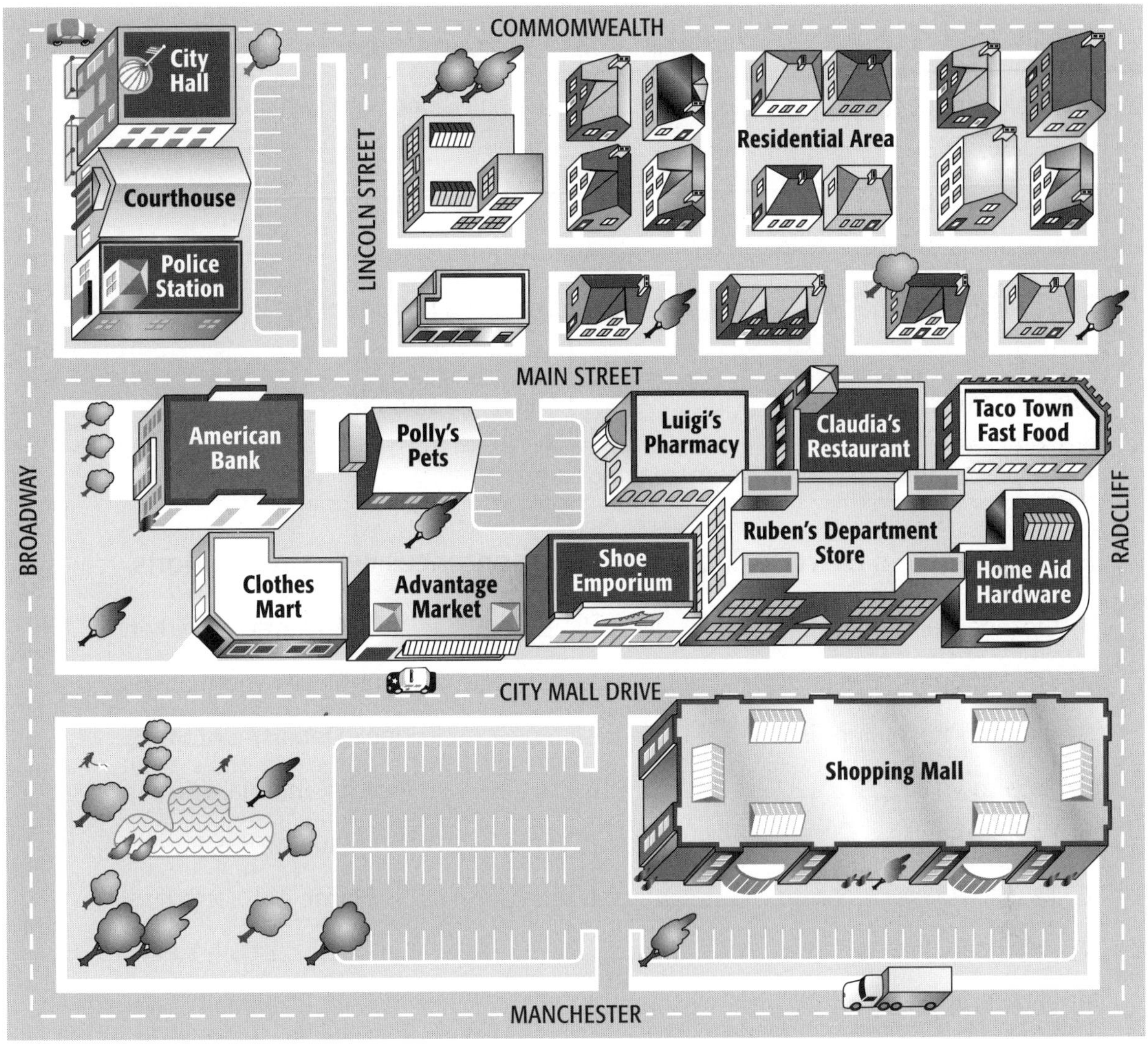

1. What is on the right of Shoe Emporium? Ruben's Department Store
2. What is on the right of Luigi's Pharmacy? __________
3. What is on the left of Luigi's Pharmacy? __________
4. What is on the right of Claudia's Restaurant? __________

C. Practice the conversation with locations from the map in Exercise B.

Student A: Excuse me. I'm lost. Can you help me?
Student B: Sure. How can I help you?
Student A: Where's <u>Polly's Pets</u>?
Student B: It's around the corner from Clothes Mart.

D. Look at the examples of prepositions.

Prepositions	
The ball is **in** the box. 	The ball is **between** two boxes. 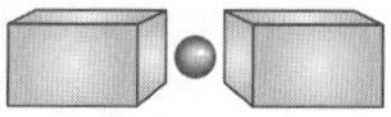
The ball is **on** the box. 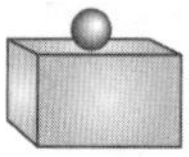	The ball is **over** the box. 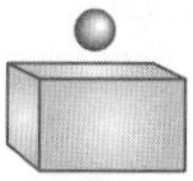
The ball is **under** the box. 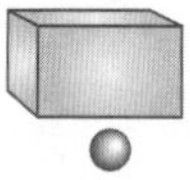	The ball is **in front of** the box. 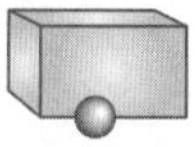
The ball is **next to** the box. 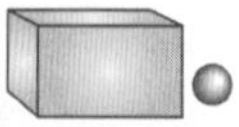	The ball is **behind** the box. 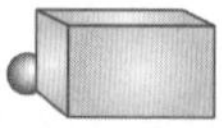
• Use prepositions to talk about where things are.	

E. Using the map in Exercise B, complete the sentences with prepositions.

1. Clothes Mart is ____next to____ Advantage Market.
2. The shopping mall is ________________ Ruben's Department Store.
3. Claudia's Restaurant is ________________ Ruben's Department Store.
4. Taco Town is ________________ Radcliff and Main Street.
5. Luigi's Pharmacy is ________________ Polly's Pets and Claudia's Restaurant.
6. Taco Town is ________________ Home Aid Hardware.
7. American Bank is ________________ Polly's Pets.
8. Shoe Emporium is ________________ City Mall Drive.
9. Shoe Emporium is ________________ Luigi's Pharmacy.
10. Polly's Pets is ________________ American Bank.

F. Write sentences about your community. Use the prepositions.

1. (next to) ________________
2. (across from) ________________
3. (between) ________________
4. (behind) ________________
5. (in front of) ________________
6. (on the corner of) ________________
7. (around the corner from) ________________

UNIT 5

LESSON 4 Please call

GOAL ■ Leave a phone message

A. Read the messages and complete the charts.

Message 1

Antonia: Please leave a message after the tone.

Alex: Hi, Antonia. I just got in to town. I want to say happy birthday. My number is 555-9786. I can't wait to see you. Bye.

Message 2

Antonia: Please leave a message after the tone.

Medical Receptionist: This is Dr. Pearson's office. You have a check-up at 9:00 a.m. tomorrow. Please call if you can't make it. Our number is 555-8207.

Message 3

Antonia: Please leave a message after the tone.

Natalie: Hi, Antonia. This is Natalie. Wow, what a great day! I want to talk to you. My number is 555-1162.

Message 4

Antonia: Please leave a message after the tone.

Antonia's Mother: Antonia, you never call me! Please call back. Call me so we can get together. The number here is 555-8947, Room 203.

PHONE MESSAGE 1
Name: ______________________
Phone Number: ______________________
Reason for Calling: ______________________
____

PHONE MESSAGE 2
Name: ______________________
Phone Number: ______________________
Reason for Calling: ______________________
____

PHONE MESSAGE 3
Name: ______________________
Phone Number: ______________________
Reason for Calling: ______________________
____

PHONE MESSAGE 4
Name: ______________________
Phone Number: ______________________
Reason for Calling: ______________________
____

B. **Look at the message and answer the questions**

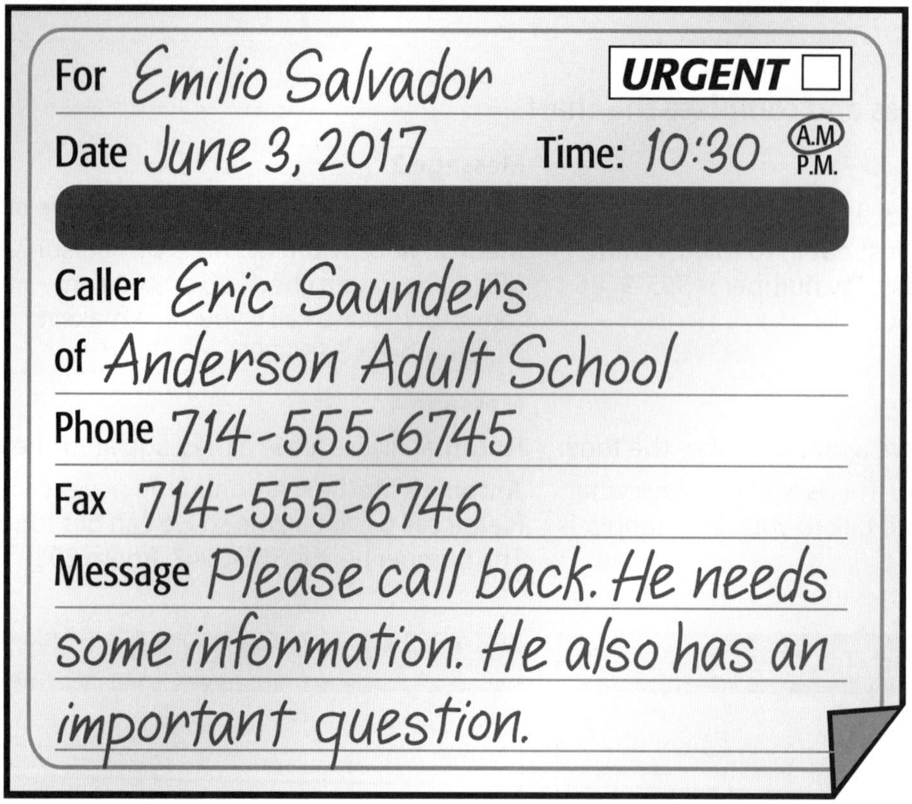

1. Who is the call for? ______Emilio Salvador______
2. Who is calling? ____________________
3. When did Eric call? ____________________
4. What is Eric's phone number? ____________________
5. What does Eric need? ____________________

C. **Read the chart.**

Questions with *Can*			
Can	Subject	Base	Example question
Can	I you	help ask talk answer call	**Can** you help me? **Can** I ask you a question? **Can** I talk to you? **Can** you answer a question? **Can** you call me?

D. Put the words in the correct order to form questions.

1. you / can / help / I Can I help you? ______
2. can / you / the teacher / talk / to ______
3. I / can / your questions / answer ______
4. see / you / can / I / tomorrow ______
5. a question / I / can / you / ask ______
6. call / you / can / I ______

E. Rewrite the sentences as questions.

1. You can answer the phones. Can you answer the phones? ______
2. I can talk to you now. ______
3. You can help me. ______
4. You can ask questions. ______
5. I can send packages in the mail. ______
6. You can ask for information. ______

F. Write the conversation in the correct order.

John: Yes. I can talk to you then.
Silvia: OK.
John: Can you call me tomorrow?
John: Hello Silvia. Can you help me?
Silvia: OK. Can I call at 3:00?
Silvia: Of course. What can I do to help?

John: Hello Silvia. Can you help me?
Silvia: ______
John: ______
Silvia: ______
John: ______
Silvia: ______

G. Write out a message you could leave on an answering machine for a friend.

1. You need to talk: ______
2. You have a question: ______
3. You want to answer a question: ______

UNIT 5

LESSON 5 Dear Mom

GOAL ■ Write an e-mail

A. Read the e-mail and complete the sentences.

Dear Ruben,

How are you? I am fine. I am writing you this letter because I want to tell you about my new neighborhood. I live in Angle Creek, Minnesota. I go to school almost every day. I often walk to school. I sometimes eat lunch around the corner from the school.
I am studying English in school. I am learning to read and write in English. The students help me study. I always read the book and I always prepare for class.

My English is good now. Can you visit me soon? I hope so.

Your friend,
Natalie

1. Natalie lives in Angle Creek, Minnesota.
2. She is studying ____________________.
3. She often ____________________ to school.

B. Answer the questions about you.

1. What street do you live on?
   I live on ____________________.
2. What do you live next to?
   I live next to ____________________.
3. What do you live around the corner from?
   I live around the corner from ____________________.
4. What do you live across from?
   I live across from ____________________.
5. Where do you like to go?
   I like to go to ____________________.

C. Write an e-mail with the sentences from Exercise B.

Dear ____________,

How are you? I want to tell you about where I live.

____

____

____

____

____

____

____

____

See you soon!

____

D. Read the charts.

Simple Present			
Subject	**Adverb**	**Verb**	**Example sentence**
I	always often sometimes rarely never	write	I always **write** postcards.
You, We, They		read	They never **read** the newspaper.
He, She, It		eat	He rarely **eats** here.

100%		50%		0%
always	often	sometimes	rarely	never

Present Continuous				
Subject	***Be***	**Base +*ing***		**Example sentence**
I	am (I'm)	writing	right now today	**I'm writing** a letter right now.
You, We, They	are (They're)	reading		They**'re reading** a book today.
He, She, It	is (She's)	eating		She**'s eating** a sandwich.

E. Look at the pictures and complete the sentences.

Present Continuous

1. The men ___are wearing___ suits.
2. The boy ____________ a sandwich.
3. The girls ____________________.
4. The woman ____________________.
5. The boys ____________________.
6. The man ____________________.

Simple Present

1. They ___wear___ suits to work.
2. He ______________ a sandwich for lunch.
3. They always ______________ in the mall.
4. She often ______________ in a chair.
5. They ______________ during recess.
6. He sometimes ____________ a newspaper.

F. Ask a partner the questions about the pictures in Exercise E.

Student A: What are the men wearing?
Student B: They are **wearing** suits.

Student A: What is the boy eating?
Student B:

Student A: What do the men wear to work?
Student B:

Student A: What does the man read?
Student B:

Student B: Where is the woman sitting?
Student A: She is **sitting** in a chair.

Student B: What do the boys do at recess?
Student A:

Student B: What is the man doing?
Student A:

Student B: Where do the girls walk?
Student A:

G. Complete the paragraph about you and your community.

Dear ____________,

How are you? I am fine. I want to tell you about my neighborhood. I live in ____________. Right now I am going to school at ____________. My class starts at ____________. I always ____________ to school. I ____________ English.

PRACTICE TEST

A. Read the questions. Circle the correct answers.

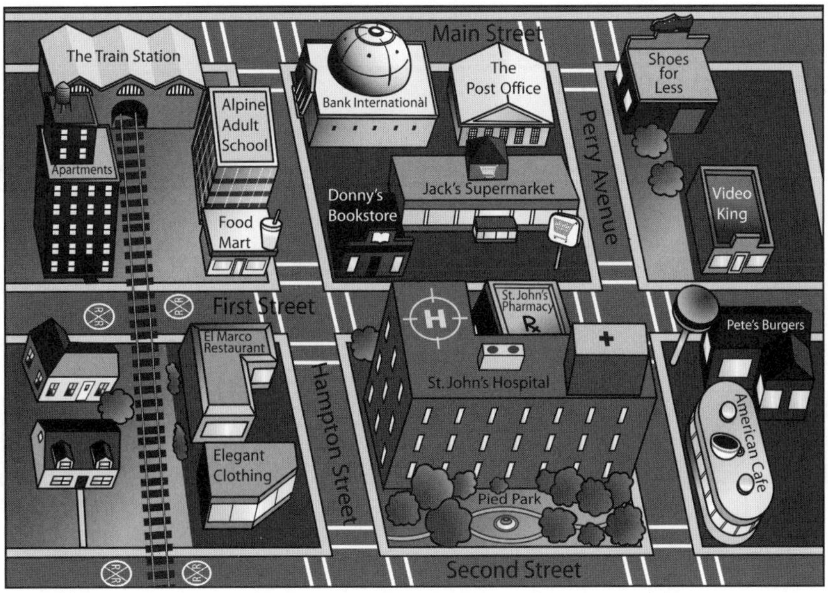

1. What is next to Jack's Supermarket?
   a. Shoes for Less b. Food Mart
   c. Pete's Burgers d. Donny's Bookstore

2. Go straight ahead. Turn right on Hampton Street. Go straight ahead. Turn left on Main Street. Where are you?
   a. The train station b. El Marco Restaurant
   c. Alpine Adult School d. The bank

3. Turn around. Turn left on Perry. Turn right on Main Street. Stop on the right. Where are you?
   a. Video King b. Food Mart
   c. Donny's Bookstore d. Shoes for Less

4. Who is the package for?
   a. Familia Ramirez b. Gabriela Ramirez
   c. Argentina d. Landsbury, WA

5. Who is the package from?
   a. Familia Ramirez b. Gabriela Ramirez
   c. Argentina d. Landsbury, WA

6. What is the street address of the sender?
   a. Av. Calao 423 b. Buenos Aires
   c. 37 Main Street d. 99037

UNIT 6

LESSON 1 Parts of the body

GOAL ■ Identify parts of the body

A. Put the words from the box into the chart.

arms	eyes	legs	stomach
back	feet	mouth	teeth
chest	hands	neck	
ears	head	nose	

Above Shoulders (A)	Below Shoulders Above Waist (B)	Below Waist (C)

B. Unscramble the body part words.

1. resa ____ears____
2. motshac ____________
3. hotum ____________
4. shnad ____________
5. reshsoldu ____________
6. staiw ____________

C. Read the paragraph and label the pictures with names from the box.

Gilberto	Marie	Hiep

I am a doctor. I see patients every day. Today I see three people, Marie, Gilberto, and Hiep. They all have problems. Marie has problems with her throat, ears, and head. The throat is down the mouth. Gilberto has problems with his legs, hips, and back. Hips are on the side of the waist. Hiep has pain in his head, eyes, and sinuses. Sinuses are mostly in the nose area.

Pain: legs, hips, back

Name: ______________

Pain: throat, ears, head

Name: ______________

Pain: head, eyes, sinuses

Name: ______________

D. Read the chart.

Simple Present: *Hurt*		
Subject	**Verb**	**Example sentence**
It My leg My arm My foot My head	hurts	My leg **hurts**. My arm **hurts**. My head **hurts**.
They My legs My arms My feet My ears	hurt	My legs **hurt**. My feet **hurt**. My ears **hurt**.

E. Circle the correct word.

1. My back **hurt** / **hurts**. I think I need to rest.
2. His legs **hurt** / **hurts**. He needs aspirin.
3. I think there is a problem with the food. My stomach **hurt** / **hurts**.
4. The doctor says I have the flu. That is why my head **hurt** / **hurts**.
5. I am reading a very long book. My eyes **hurt** / **hurts**.
6. I am walking to school. It is difficult because my legs **hurt** / **hurts**.
7. Jason's ears **hurt** / **hurts**. I think he needs to see the doctor.
8. I am wearing new shoes and my feet **hurt** / **hurts**.

F. Complete the information about Gilberto, Marie, and Hiep from Exercise C.

	Pain		
Gilberto	legs	hips	back
Marie			
Hiep			

G. Write sentences about Gilberto, Marie, and Hiep.

1. Gilberto's hips hurt.
2. Marie ______________________.
3. Her ______________________.
4. Hiep's ______________________.
5. His ______________________.
6. His ______________________.
7. Gilberto's ______________________.

UNIT 6

LESSON 2 What's the problem?

GOAL ■ Identify illnesses and health problems

A. Study the chart with the symptoms. Read the sentences. Then, write the name in the chart below.

Common cold symptoms	Common flu symptoms
low fever	high fever
sore throat	sore throat
headache	headache
runny nose	muscle aches
	dry cough

1. Michael has a sore throat and a high fever.
2. Eduardo has a low fever.
3. Kambu has a headache and a dry cough.
4. Lily has a runny nose.
5. Maria has a cough.
6. Norman has a high fever and his muscles ache.
7. Quang's muscles ache.
8. Laura has a sore throat and a runny nose.

Who do you think has a cold?	Who do you think has the flu?
	Michael

B. **Read the graph.**

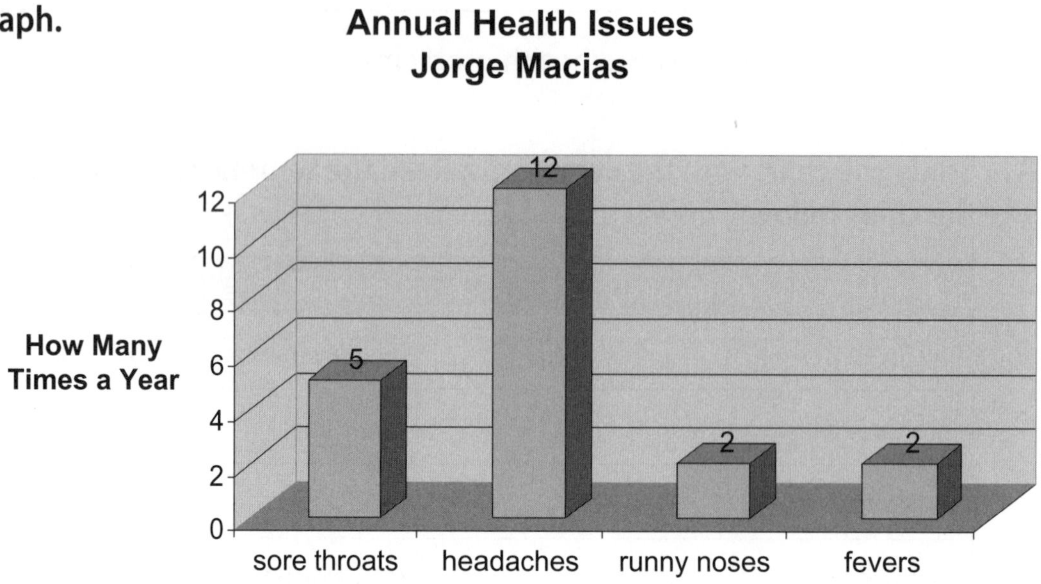

C. **Answer the questions about Jorge.**

1. How many headaches does Jorge have every year? ___12___
2. How many sore throats does he have? ____________
3. How many fevers does he have? ____________
4. How many runny noses does he have? ____________

D. **Read the charts.**

Affirmative Simple Present: *Have*		
Subject	***Have***	**Example sentence**
I, You, We, They	have	I **have** a headache. You **have** a sore throat.
He, She, It	has	She **has** a stomachache. He **has** a fever.

Negative Simple Present: *Have*			
Subject	**Negative**	***Have***	**Example sentence**
I, You, We, They	do not (don't)	have	I **don't have** a headache. You **don't have** a sore throat.
He, She, It	does not (doesn't)	have	She **doesn't have** a stomachache. He **doesn't have** a fever.

E. Circle the correct word.

1. Guillermo's head hurts. He **has** / **have** a headache.
2. Omar's back hurts. He **has / have** a backache.
3. My throat hurts. I **has / have** a sore throat.
4. We need a doctor. We **has / have** stomachaches.
5. My children are sick. They **has / have** earaches.
6. I don't need a doctor. I don't **has / have** a headache.
7. She is very healthy. She **don't / doesn't** have any problems.
8. I think it is a cold. You don't **have / has** a fever.

F. Rewrite the sentences in the negative simple present.

1. They have a fever. *They don't have a fever.*
2. She has a sore throat. ______________________
3. We have colds. ______________________
4. I have a stomachache. ______________________
5. Marco has a headache. ______________________
6. You have the flu. ______________________

G. Read the information.

Symptom	Guillermo	Antonio	Maritza
sore throat	three times a year	two times a year	four times a year
headache	one time a year	twenty times a year	ten times a year
runny nose	two times a year	six times a year	eight times a year
fever	one time a year	four times a year	three times a year

H. Write sentences using the information in Exercise G.

1. *Guillermo has a sore throat three times a year.*
2. ______________________
3. ______________________
4. ______________________

UNIT 6

LESSON 3 What should I do?

GOAL ■ Give advice

A. Match the symptom to the medicine. Draw lines.

headache

sore throat

cough

upset stomach

B. Write sentences about what you need.

1. I have a headache. I need ______________________
2. I have a sore throat. ______________________
3. I have a cough. ______________________
4. I have an upset stomach. ______________________

C. Read the medicine labels.

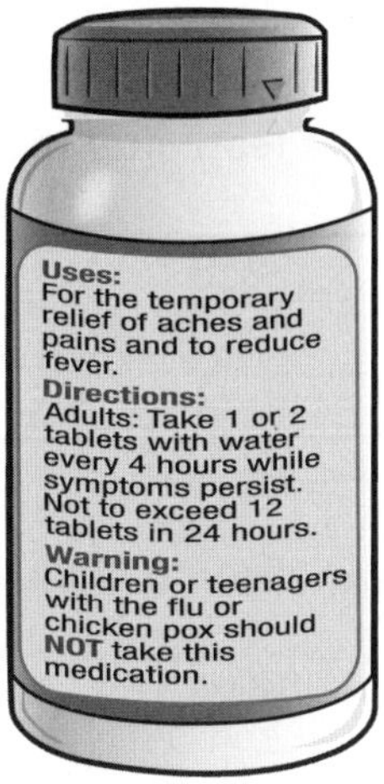

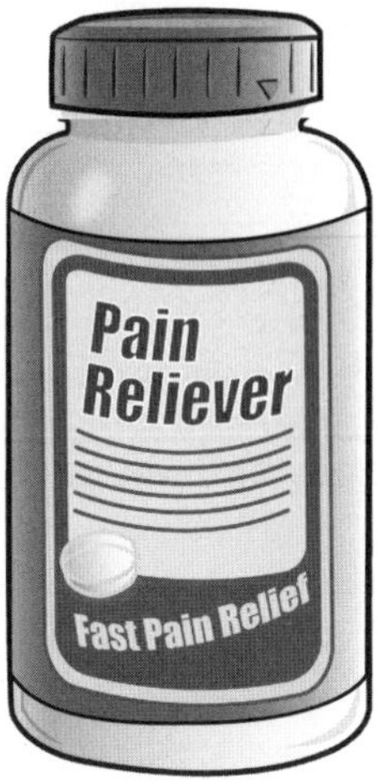

D. Circle the best answers.

1. How many tablets do adults take?
   a. 2 to 3
   b. 1 to 2
   c. four hours

2. Children with the flu should not take it.
   a. true
   b. false

3. What is this medicine for?
   a. for runny noses
   b. for aches and pains
   c. for stomachaches

4. You can take 24 tablets in one day.
   a. true
   b. false

E. Read the charts.

Modal: *Should*			
Subject	***Should***	**Base verb**	**Example sentence**
I, You, He, She, It, We, They	should	rest stay go take	You **should** rest. He **should** stay home. They **should** go to the doctor. I **should** take pain relievers. We **should** take cough syrup.

Modal: *Should* (Negative)			
Subject	***Should***	**Base verb**	**Example sentence**
I, You, He, She, It, We, They	should not (shouldn't)	drive drink go	You **shouldn't drive** and take this medicine. He **shouldn't drink** alcohol with this medicine. We **shouldn't go** out.

F. Complete the sentences.

1. She ___should eat___ (eat) after taking this medicine.
2. You ______________ (get) a lot of sleep and rest.
3. They ______________ (no/take) the medicine if they have the flu.
4. Nancy and Margie ______________ (no/drink) when taking this medicine.
5. I ______________ (no/go) to work. I am sick.
6. We ______________ (take) two tablets three times a day.
7. Karen ______________ (take) cough syrup for her sore throat.
8. He ______________ (see) a doctor right now.

G. Read the labels and complete the sentences with *should* or *shouldn't*.

COUGH SYRUP

Usage: For temporary relief of cough and sore throat irritation due to infections.

Directions: Take two teaspoons every four hours for pain.

***Warning:* Don't take if you are pregnant.**

Antacid Tablets

Usage: For fast relief of acid indigestion and stomach pain.

Directions: Take two to four tablets as needed.

***Warning:* Don't give this medicine to children.**

1. I see you have a cough. You ______________ take some cough syrup.
2. Oh, you have an upset stomach. You ______________ take antacid.
3. Be careful! You ______________ take cough syrup if you are pregnant.
4. You ______________ give antacid to children.
5. You ______________ take two teaspoons every four hours.
6. You ______________ take six tablets.

H. Complete the chart. What medicines should you take?

Headache	Stomachache	Sore throat	Aches and pains	Cough

UNIT 6

LESSON 4 There's an emergency!

GOAL ■ Ask for information

A. Read the conversation. Write two new conversations with the information in the chart below.

911: 911, how can I help you?
Bao: My father is having a heart attack.
911: What's your name?
Bao: Bao Tran.
911: OK, Bao, where is your father?
Bao: 5946 Beach Blvd.
911: That's 5946 Beach Blvd., right?
Bao: That's right.
911: The ambulance is on its way.

Who	What	Where
Bao Tran	My father is having a heart attack.	5946 Beach Blvd
Michelle Khalili	My daughter broke her arm.	84631 Second Street
Susan McClellan	Our house is on fire.	36 Hermosa Street

911: ______________________
Michelle: ______________________
911: ______________________
Michelle: ______________________
911: ______________________
Michelle: ______________________
911: ______________________
Michelle: ______________________
911: ______________________

911: ______________________
Susan: ______________________
911: ______________________
Susan: ______________________
911: ______________________
Susan: ______________________
911: ______________________
Susan: ______________________
911: ______________________

B. Read the paragraph.

There is a house on fire at 2245 Adam Street in Costa Mesa. It is an emergency. There are three people in the house and the firefighters are helping them. The fire is very hot. The three people are Jim, Kathy, and Lucy Hamilton. It is now 3:30 p.m. and the fire is intense!

C. Complete the sentences about the fire.

1. Jim, Kathy, and Lucy Hamilton live at 2245 Adam Street.
2. The fire is in the city of ______________________.
3. It is ______________________ in the afternoon.
4. ______________________ people are in the house.
5. The firefighters are helping ______________________, ______________________, and ______________________.

D. Read the chart.

Question word	Verb	Example question	Example answer
What	is	**What** is the emergency?	There is a fire! There is an accident. A house is on fire. My father is having a heart attack.
Where	is	**Where** is the emergency?	On First Street. Here in my house. At 1432 W. Palm Street.
Who	is calling is talking is in trouble	**Who** is calling? **Who** is talking? **Who** is in trouble?	John. John. My father, Eric Ludlow.

E. Fill in the blank with the correct word. Use *Who, What,* or *Where*.

1. <u>Where</u> is the fire? It's on First Street, next to the market.
2. ________ is the problem? My son has a broken arm.
3. ________ is the emergency? We need assistance. There is a car accident.
4. ________ is in trouble? My brother is having a heart attack.
5. ________ is the accident? It is on the corner of Maple and Birch Street.
6. ________ is calling? My name is Roger Dunn.
7. ________ is the matter? My house is on fire!

F. Read the emergency calls.

1. A house is on fire at 3234 Maple Street. My name is Claudia. Please hurry!

2. I am Greg LeBonte. I live on Sycamore Street. There is a car in my living room!

3. There is an accident on Main Street and McFadden. Please hurry. My name is Annabelle and my phone number is 555-6754.

4. Please send the paramedics immediately to 7774 W. Harbor Blvd. My father is having a heart attack. His name is Oscar Mejia.

G. Complete the chart with the information from Exercise F.

Who	What	Where
1. Claudia	house on fire	3234 Maple Street
2.		
3.		
4.		

H. Write a new emergency call. Use Exercise F as a model.

UNIT 6

LESSON 5 Staying healthy

GOAL ■ Develop an exercise plan

A. Read about John and Maria. Then, complete the Venn diagram.

John exercises every day. He has many goals. He wants to lose weight and be healthy. He runs two miles in the morning and goes to the gym in the evening. He rides a bicycle to work three days a week.

Maria exercises three days a week. She has many goals. She wants to lose weight and be healthy. She runs in the morning and walks in the evening. She also walks at lunch.

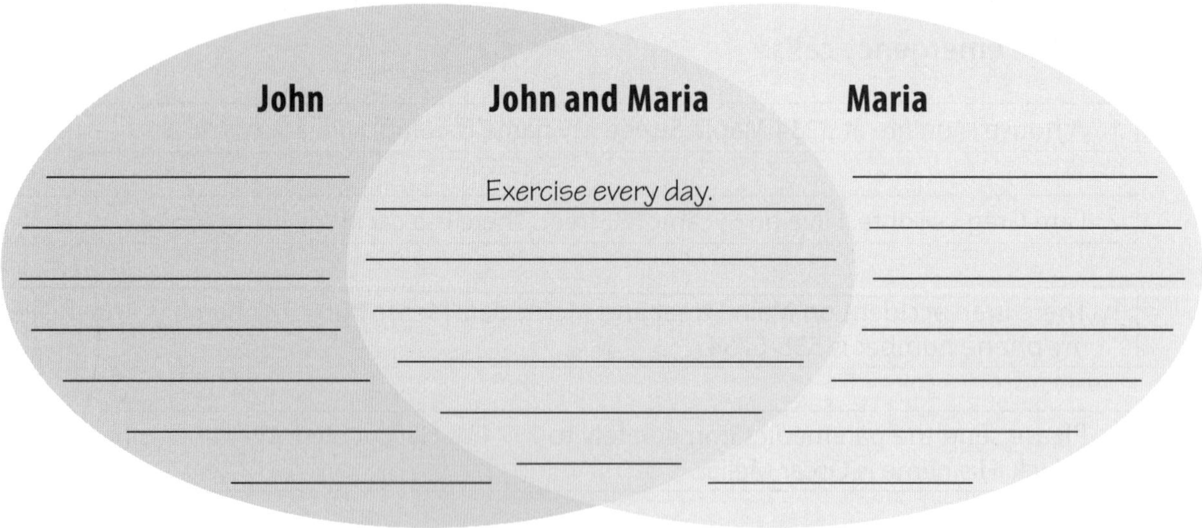

B. Read the bar graph and answer the questions.

Alta, Wisconsin (Average Sleep Per Night)

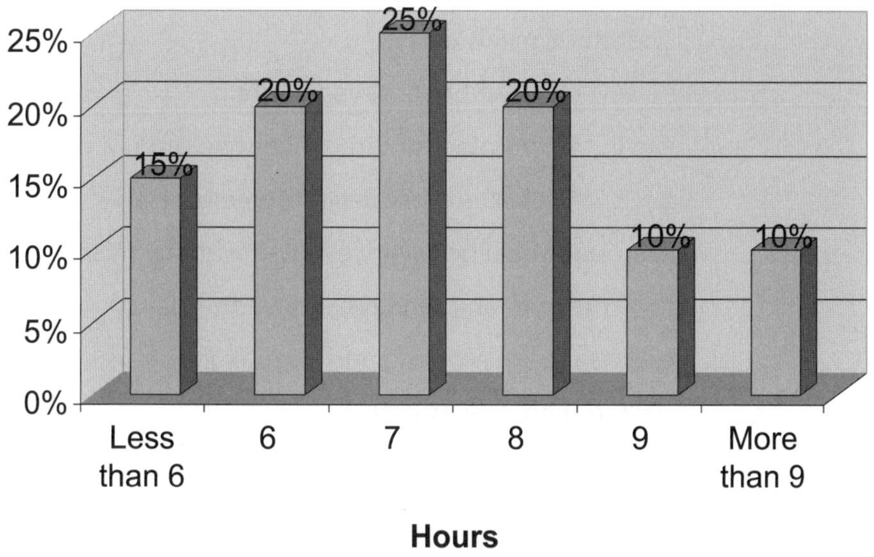

1. What percentage of people sleep seven hours every night? 25%
2. What percentage of people sleep more than nine hours? ____________
3. What percentage of people sleep six hours every night? ____________
4. How many hours do you sleep? ____________
5. What number of hours is healthy? ____________

C. Read the chart.

Want to				
Subject	**Verb**	**Infinitive (*to* + base)**		**Example sentence**
I, You, We, They	want	to	run exercise walk	I **want to run.** We **want to exercise.** They **want to walk.**
He, She, It	wants		ride do go eat sleep	He **wants to ride** a bicycle. She **wants to do** yard work. She **wants to go** to the gym. Oscar **wants to eat** three meals a day. Maria **wants to sleep** eight hours a night.

D. Write *want to* or *wants to*.

1. The woman _____wants to_____ exercise one hour every day.
2. We __________ make goals for our health.
3. They __________ eat three meals a day.
4. I __________ sleep seven or eight hours every night.
5. Luz __________ run in the morning for three miles two times a week.
6. Paula and I __________ ride bikes every day for three miles.
7. I __________ walk around the block every evening with my husband.
8. He __________ go to the gym on Mondays and Wednesdays.
9. Eva __________ exercise in the morning and sleep eight hours at night.
10. We __________ walk to school every day.

E. Read the goal chart.

Name	Sleep	Exercise	Meals
Martha	8 hours	20 minutes	3 meals
Kimberly	7 hours	1 hour	2 meals
Luis	7 hours	45 minutes	3 meals

F. Write sentences about the goals in Exercise E.

1. Martha wants to sleep eight hours every night.
2. Martha __________.
3. Martha __________.
4. Kimberly and Luis __________.
5. Martha and Luis __________.

G. What are your goals for sleep, meals, and exercise? Write your goals and your partner's goals. Then, report to a group.

1. I want to __________.
2. __________
3. __________
4. My partner wants to __________.
5. __________
6. __________

PRACTICE TEST

A. Read the paragraph and look at the pictures. Circle the correct answers.

My Health
by Miyuki Tanaka

I am healthy. I eat well and rarely get sick. I was sick one time last year. I had a cold. I had a headache and a runny nose, and I was tired a lot. I had the cold for 10 days.

I exercise two times a day. I exercise in the morning for 20 minutes and I walk in the evening for 20 minutes every day. I drink a lot of water, take vitamins, and eat three meals a day. I think that I am very healthy.

1. How much does Miyuki exercise?
   a. two times a day b. only in the evening
   c. drinks lots of water d. takes vitamins

2. How long was her cold last year?
   a. tired a lot b. runny nose
   c. headache d. 10 days

3. What were Miyuki's symptoms?
   a. headache, runny nose, tired b. 20 minutes every day
   c. sick d. vitamins

4. What medicine is for a sore throat?
   a. pain reliever b. cough syrup
   c. throat lozenges d. none

5. What medicine is for back pain?
   a. pain reliever b. cough syrup
   c. throat lozenges d. none

6. How much cough syrup do you take every time?
   a. 2 tablespoons b. 1 throat lozenge
   c. every four hours d. every three hours

pain reliever

cough syrup

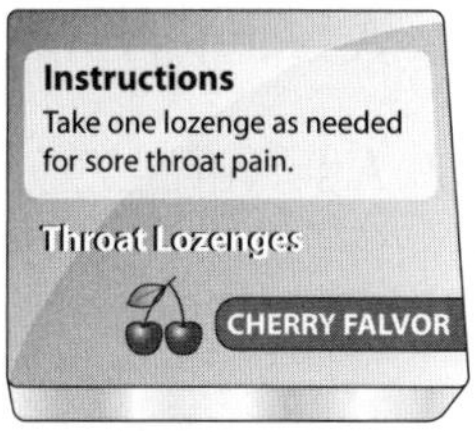

throat lozenges

UNIT 7

LESSON 1 What's your job?

GOAL ■ Identify common occupations

A. Write where the people work in the right column. Use the words in the box below. You can use some words more than once.

doctor's office	office/office building	school
garage	restaurant	store
hospital		

Job title	Where they work
cashier	*restaurant, store*
cook	
custodian	
doctor	
nurse	
secretary	
server	
teacher	

B. Write sentences about the chart in Exercise A.

1. A cashier works *in a restaurant or a store* .
2. A cook works ________________.
3. A custodian works ________________.
4. A doctor works ________________.
5. A nurse works ________________.
6. A secretary works ________________.
7. A server ________________.
8. A teacher ________________.

C. Read the information.

Natalia is a carpenter.

Esteban is a delivery person.

Kristina is a computer programmer.

Phuong is a homemaker.

D. List the inside and outside jobs.

Inside	Outside

E. List jobs that require special education.

Special education	No special education

F. Read the charts.

Affirmative Simple Present		
Subject	Verb	Example sentence
I, You, We, They	work	I **work**. I **work** inside. We **work** in an office. They **work** in a store.
He, She, It	works	He **works** outside. She **works** inside.

Negative Simple Present			
Subject	Negative	Verb	Example sentence
I, You, We, They	don't	work	I **don't work** outside. We **don't work** in an office. They **don't work** in a store.
He, She, It	doesn't	work	He **doesn't work** in an office. She **doesn't work** in a store.

G. Complete the sentences with the correct form of *work*.

1. Ramiro is a doctor. He ___doesn't work___ in a supermarket.
2. The brothers are mechanics. They ______________ at Adel's Clothing.
3. I am an assembler. I ______________ in a factory.
4. We are homemakers. We ______________ at Centennial Adult School.
5. You are a babysitter. You ______________ with children.
6. Ly sleeps from 6:00 a.m.–12:00 p.m. She ______________ in the evening.

H. Read the information.

Name	Store	Factory	Office	Outside	Car	Home
Chen, Alan, and Oscar		×				
Benjamin	×					
Tien			×			
Peter and Sally				×		
Tino, Maria, and Gaspar						×
Ron					×	

I. Write sentences about where the people in Exercise H work.

1. Chen, Alan, and Oscar ___work in a factory___.
2. Benjamin ______________.
3. Tien ______________.
4. Peter and Sally ______________.
5. Tino, Maria, and Gaspar ______________.
6. Ron ______________.

J. Write information about three family members.

____

____

____

____

UNIT 7

LESSON 2 Job hunting

GOAL ■ Interpret job information

A. Read the job announcement from the Internet and answer the questions.

Lonnie's Real Estate

Position: Secretary

Location: 145 W. Maple St., Olton Park

Wages: $22

Full- or Part-Time: Full-Time

Summary:
Responsible for writing letters, filing, and speaking to clients. Must be friendly. Must speak English. Two years experience required.

Essential Functions:

- Writes memos
- Manages files
- Speaks to clients (customers)

Benefits

- 1 week vacation annually
- medical insurance
- 6 sick days annually

APPLY NOW

1. What is the job title?
   a. secretary   b. full-time   c. two years experience

2. How much is the pay?
   a. full-time   b. 6 sick days   c. $22

3. What is a "client"?
   a. speak English   b. a customer   c. Olton Park

4. What is annually?
   a. 1 week   b. 6 days   c. every year

B. Read the classified ads and complete the table.

DAILY NEWS *Classified Ads*

EMPLOYMENT

Apartment Manager
FT, 2 yrs exp, free rent, speak Spanish and English, paint and minor maintenance. Available immediately.
Call Manor Apartments, 555-8976.

Full-Time Cook
No experience needed, training available, Martha's Kitchen, good hours, apply in person, 3456 W. Melrose, Hill City, 8am-5pm

Legal Assistant
45 wpm, filing, speak English, FT, great opportunity, Smith and Peterson Law Office. Call 555-9988.

Position	Experience?	FT or PT
Apartment Manager		

C. Read the charts.

Modal: *Can* (Ability)			
Subject	***Can***	**Verb**	**Example sentence**
I, You, He, She, It, We, They	can	drive speak talk collect clean	I **can** drive a truck. You **can** speak English well. He **can** talk to customers. We **can** collect money. They **can** clean the offices.

Can (Negative)			
Subject	***Can***	**Verb**	**Example sentence**
I, You, He, She, It, We, They	cannot (can't)	drive speak talk collect clean	I **can't** drive a truck. You **can't** speak English well. He **can't** talk to customers. We **can't** collect money. They **can't** clean the offices.

D. Each sentence contains a mistake. Rewrite the sentences correctly with *can*.

1. He cans drive a truck. He can drive a truck.
2. My sister can to calculate numbers quickly. ____________________
3. She cans type very well. ____________________
4. She can in a factory work. ____________________
5. They no can talk on the phone. ____________________
6. Miyuki no work outside. ____________________

E. Look at the diagram.

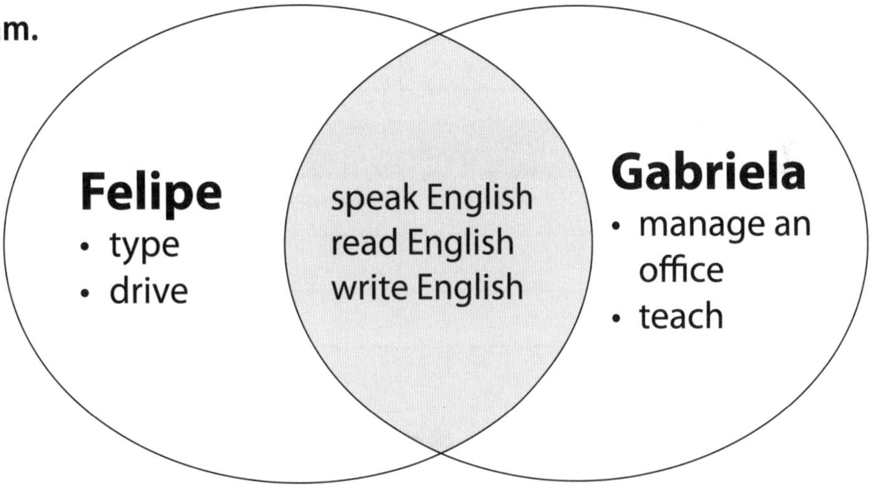

F. Write sentences about what Felipe and Gabriela *can* and *can't* do.

1. Felipe can type letters.
2. Felipe can't ____________________.
3. Gabriela can ____________________.
4. Gabriela can't ____________________.
5. Felipe and Gabriela can ____________________.
6. Felipe and Gabriela can ____________________.

G. Write what you *can* and *can't* do.

____

____

UNIT 7

LESSON 3 What was your job before?

GOAL ■ Write your job history

A. Write Sam's job history. Write the most recent (last) job first.

Job History
Sam Jennings

Position	Company	From	To	Duties
Server	Allen's Café	6-2000	8-2003	served customers
Assistant Manager	Allen's Café	8-2003	1-2007	helped manager
Manager	Allen's Café	1-2007	present	supervises workers

Position	Company	From	To	Duties

B. Write Ogal's job history. Write the most recent (last) job first.

Job History
Ogal Claspell

Position	Company	From	To	Duties
Custodian	Tyndale Department Stores	1-1996	8-2004	cleaned offices
Teacher	Lincoln Adult School	8-2004	1-2014	taught adult students English
Principal	Lincoln Adult School	1- 2014	present	supervises teachers

Position	Company	From	To	Duties

C. Read Nathan's job history section of an application.

POSITION	COMPANY	FROM	TO	DUTIES (responsibilities)
Supervisor	Archer's Furniture	05-2012	05-2016	managed ten workers
Delivery Person	Archer's Furniture	01-2009	04-2012	delivered furniture
Assembler	Tricon Industries	10-2007	01 -2009	assembled parts to radios

D. Answer the questions about the job history in Exercise C.

1. Where did Nathan work in 2010? Nathan worked at Archer's Furniture.
2. When did he work in Tricon Industries? ______________________________
3. What job did he have in May 2012? ______________________________
4. What were his responsibilities in 2008? ______________________________

E. Read the charts.

Simple Past: Regular Verbs			
Subject	**Base + *ed***		**Example sentence**
I, You, He, She, It, We, They	cleaned cooked prepared delivered counted helped moved	tables hamburgers breakfast packages the money other workers to the United States	I **cleaned** tables. You **cooked** hamburgers. He **prepared** breakfast. She **delivered** packages. It **counted** the money. We **helped** other workers. They **moved** to the United States.

Simple Past: *Be*			
Subject	***Be***		**Example sentence**
I, He, She, It	was	a mail carrier	I **was** a mail carrier.
We, You, They	were	happy	You **were** happy.

F. Complete the sentences with the correct simple past tense form of the verbs.

1. I ___was___ a mechanic. I ___repaired___ (repair) cars.
2. She ____________ an assembly worker. She ____________ (assemble) furniture.
3. We ____________ mail carriers. We ____________ (deliver) mail.
4. You ____________ a secretary. You ____________ (type) letters.
5. They ____________ servers at a restaurant. They ____________ (talk) to customers.
6. Juana and I ____________ managers. We ____________ (supervise) workers.
7. Sherrie ____________ a cook. She ____________ (cook) food for La Roma Restaurant.
8. You ____________ a cashier. You ____________ (count) money for the store.

G. Read the information.

Name	Before	Now
Mario	office worker / type letters	student / study English
Gabriela	teacher / help students	writer / write books
Rex	mechanic / repair cars	driver / drive a taxi
Pam	mail carrier / deliver letters	salesperson / sell computers

H. Write sentences with the information in Exercise G.

1. Mario ___is a student. He studies English. He was an office worker. He typed letters___.
2. Gabriela ____
____.
3. Rex ____
____.
4. Pam ____
____.

I. Complete a job history for you.

Position	Company	From	To	Duties (responsibilities)

LESSON 4 A job interview

GOAL ■ Perform a job interview

A. Match the interview statements with the person being interviewed (interviewee).

Interviewer	Interviewee
Can I help you?	I don't work right now.
Do you have experience?	I worked at Hamilton Flowers. I was a salesperson.
Do you speak English?	Thank you.
I am Mr. Tuttle. Please sit down.	Yes, a little. I'm studying in school.
Where did you work before?	No, but I learn quickly.
Where do you work now?	Yes, thank you. I am here for the cashier position. Is Mr. Tuttle here?

B. Make a conversation with the questions and answers in Exercise A.

Interviewer: *Can I help you?*

Interviewee: *Yes, thank you. I am here for the cashier position. Is Mr. Tuttle here?*

Interviewer: ____________________

Interviewee: ____________________

Interviewer: ____________________

Interviewee: ____________________

Interviewer: ____________________

Interviewee: ____________________

Interviewer: ____________________

Interviewee: ____________________

Interviewer: ____________________

Interviewee: ____________________

C. Read the information and circle *True* or *False*.

Job	Mops	Answers phones	Talks to customers	Types letters	Takes breaks	Files papers
Salesperson		x	x		x	
Administrative Assistant		x		x	x	x
Receptionist		x	x		x	x
Custodian	x				x	

1. A salesperson sometimes answers phones.
   True
   False
2. A receptionist mops the floor.
   True
   False
3. An administrative assistant types.
   True
   False
4. A custodian files papers.
   True
   False
5. A salesperson talks to customers.
   True
   False
6. A receptionist types letters.
   True
   False

D. Read the chart.

Questions with *Can*			
Can	**Subject**	**Verb**	**Example questions and answers**
Can	I, you, he, she, it, we, they	type drive talk work understand cook clean	**Can** you type letters? Yes, I can. **Can** they drive a car? No, they can't. **Can** she understand English? Yes, she can. **Can** I work on Saturdays? Yes, you can. **Can** he cook breakfast? No, he can't. **Can** we clean on the weekend? Yes, you can. **Can** you talk to customers? No, you can't.

E. Make questions with the words and *can*.

1. type / you / letters ____Can you type letters?____
2. speak / they / English ________________
3. I / work / every week ________________
4. we / talk / to the supervisor ________________
5. clean / bathrooms / you ________________
6. repair / she / my car ________________

F. Complete the conversation with the correct words.

Business Owner:	It is nice to meet you, Javier.
Javier:	It is nice to meet you, too.
Business Owner:	We need a custodian and repair person.
Javier:	Yes, I know. I ____________ clean and I ____________ do plumbing.
Business Owner:	That's great. ____________ you repair windows and doors?
Javier:	Yes, I ____________.
Business Owner:	You need to complete reports. ____________ you ____________ in English?
Javier:	No, I am sorry. I am studying English in school, but I ____________ ask my teacher for help with the forms.
Business Owner:	Yes, I think we ____________ work with that.
Javier:	Thank you.

G. Answer the questions. Write *Yes, I can* or *No, I can't*.

1. Can you type? ________________
2. Can you drive? ________________
3. Can you file papers? ________________
4. Can you clean offices? ________________
5. Can you speak English? ________________
6. Can you answer phones? ________________

UNIT 7

LESSON 5 He's a good worker

GOAL ■ Interpret performance reviews

A. Complete the evaluation form about your study skills.

EVALUATION FORM

Date: ______________________________

School: ______________________________

Name: ______________________________

Course: ______________________________

____

Teacher: ______________________________

Comes to class on time.

Superior *Good* *Needs improvement*

Listens carefully to the teacher.

Superior *Good* *Needs improvement*

Helps other students.

Superior *Good* *Needs improvement*

Participates in class.

Superior *Good* *Needs improvement*

Does homework.

Superior *Good* *Needs improvement*

Comments / Notes:

B. Read the evaluation form. List the rating for each skill.

Fairview Hotel

Employee Evaluation Form

Employee Name: Dalva Mendes
Position: Administrative Assistant
Date: April 4

EVALUATION

1. Comes to work on time	S	**G**	NI
2. Follows instructions	**S**	G	NI
3. Helps others	**S**	G	NI
4. Works well with the team	**S**	G	NI
5. Understands the job	S	G	**NI**
New employee. She is still learning.			
6. Has a positive attitude	**S**	G	NI
Enjoys her job and is always cheerful			

Supervisor's signature: Patricia Macias
Employee's signature: Dalva Mendes

S = Superior   G = Good   NI = Needs improvement

Skill	Rating
1. Comes to work on time.	G
2. Follows instructions.	______
3. Understands the job.	______
4. Helps others.	______
5. Is a team player.	______
6. Has a positive attitude.	______

C. Read the charts.

Simple Present: *Be*			
Subject	***Be***	**Adjective**	**Example sentence**
I	am	early late punctual friendly neat and clean	I **am** always early to work.
He, She	is		She **is** sometimes late to work.
We, You, They	are		We **are** punctual after our break. You **are** rarely friendly with the customers.

Simple Past: *Be*			
Subject	***Be***	**Adjective**	**Example sentence**
I, He, She	was	early late punctual friendly neat and clean	I **was** always early to work. She **was** sometimes late to work.
We, You, They	were		We **were** punctual after our break. You **were** rarely friendly with the customers.

D. **Complete the sentences with the correct *be* verb and word from the box. Some words may be used more than once.**

early	late	punctual	friendly	neat and clean

1. Dalva is always on time. She ___is___ very ___punctual___.
2. Work starts at 7:00 a.m. Maria arrives at 6:30. She __________ always __________.
3. Last year, Kevin never arrived on time. He __________ always __________.
4. Nina is often not careful when she talks. She __________ rarely __________.
5. Look at the office. It is a mess! Olga __________ never __________.
6. Nathan works hard. He has car trouble. He __________ sometimes __________ to work.
7. Martha was good with customers. She __________ always __________ with them.
8. Jim has a problem. He doesn't clean his area. He __________ never __________.

E. **Read Dalva's evaluation.**

> Dalva is a good worker. She is usually punctual. She is rarely late to work. She likes to help others and is always very friendly. She should take a break, but she rarely does.
>
> Yesterday, I worked with Dalva. She arrived on time. She followed all instructions well. Her work area is very clean. She always answers the phone and talks to customers with a friendly smile. Yesterday, Dalva had lunch in the cafeteria. She returned to work 20 minutes early. She likes to work. Dalva is a good employee.
>
> *Patricia Macias*

F. **Complete the sentences about Dalva's evaluation in Exercise E using the correct form of the *be* verb.**

1. Dalva ___is___ usually punctual.
2. She __________ rarely late to work.
3. Dalva __________ at work on time yesterday.
4. After lunch yesterday, Dalva __________ back to work 20 minutes early.
5. Dalva's work area __________ always clean and neat.
6. Dalva __________ a good employee.

G. **Complete the sentences about you and school.**

1. I ______________________________________ to school. (late / early / on time)
2. I ______________________________________ at school. (friendly / clean and neat)

PRACTICE TEST

A. Read the information. Circle the correct answers.

Employee Evaluation Form

Date: January 15
Company: Rodman's Market

Name: Kristina Perez
Position: Cashier
Supervisor: Esther Landi

Punctuality (comes to work on time):
Needs improvement   Good   Superior
Appearance (professional dress and grooming):
Needs improvement   Good   Superior
Follows instructions:
Needs improvement   Good   Superior
Helps others:
Needs improvement   Good   Superior
Has a positive attitude:
Needs improvement   Good   Superior

1. Who is the evaluation about?
   a. Esther Landi   b. Rodman's Market   c. Kristina Perez   d. cashier
2. Where can she improve?
   a. appearance   b. follows instructions   c. helps others   d. punctuality
3. When was the evaluation?
   a. January 15   b. cashier   c. supervisor   d. has a positive attitude

JOB HISTORY

POSITION	COMPANY	FROM	TO
Administrative Assistant	Fairview Hotel	December 2007	November 2008
Cashier	La Tostada Restaurant	June 2004	November 2007

4. When was Dalva a cashier?
   a. from 2004 to 2007   b. La Tostada Restaurant   c. from 2007 to 2008   d. Fairview Hotel
5. Why did she leave the cashier job?
   a. She worked at Tostada Restaurant   b. She moved.   c. She got a new job.   d. She didn't understand English.
6. What was her last job title?
   a. cashier   b. Fairview Hotel   c. administrative assistant   d. La Tostada Restaurant

UNIT 8

LESSON 1 How are your study habits?

GOAL ■ Evaluate study habits

A. Complete the chart about you.

What do you do?	How often? *never, rarely, sometimes, a lot*
1. Write in a journal	
2. Practice English at work	
3. Practice English with friends	
4. Practice English with my family	
5. Keep a vocabulary notebook	
6. Watch TV in English	
7. Listen to the radio in English	
8. Study my book	

B. Write sentences about Exercise A.

1. I rarely write in a journal.
2. ______________________________
3. ______________________________
4. ______________________________
5. ______________________________
6. ______________________________
7. ______________________________
8. ______________________________

C. Read the story and underline the past tense verbs.

Armando worked hard and was a good student. He was always early to class. He learned a lot and he was ready for the next level. Armando spoke English every day. He watched TV, talked to people in English, and practiced all the time. He listened to the teacher's instructions carefully and he always helped the other students.

D. Read the chart.

Base form	Past form	Base form	Past form	Base form	Past form
become	became	give	gave	see	saw
begin	began	go	went	sell	sold
break	broke	grow	grew	send	sent
bring	brought	hang	hung	sing	sang
build	built	have	had	sit	sat
buy	bought	hear	heard	sleep	slept
catch	caught	hurt	hurt	speak	spoke
choose	chose	know	knew	spend	spent
come	came	leave	left	stand	stood
cost	cost	lose	lost	sweep	swept
cut	cut	make	made	take	took
do	did	meet	met	teach	taught
draw	drew	pay	paid	tell	told
drink	drank	put	put	think	thought
drive	drove	quit	quit	throw	threw
eat	ate	read	read*	understand	understood
feel	felt	ride	rode	wake	woke
find	found	ring	rang	wear	wore
forget	forgot	run	ran	write	wrote
get	got	say	said		

- Many verbs are irregular in the simple past tense. You need to memorize these verbs.

* The past form **read** rhymes with **red**.

E. Complete each sentence with the past tense of the verb in parentheses.

1. We ___built___ (build) this road last year.
2. I ____________ (hear) about the benefits.
3. We ____________ (buy) suits for the interview.
4. She ____________ (give) me my paycheck.
5. I ____________ (hurt) my knee at work.
6. Victor ____________ (wear) a hard hat.
7. She ____________ (become) a doctor.
8. The custodians ____________ (throw) out the trash.
9. My boss ____________ (catch) a cold.
10. Beth ____________ (read) her evaluation.
11. He ____________ (find) a great job.
12. She ____________ (know) every coworker.
13. I ____________ (put) the package over there.
14. We ____________ (find) the office keys.
15. He ____________ (pay) the delivery person.

F. Complete the paragraph with past tense verbs.

Christy is a great student. She works hard. She ___got___ (get) to school on time every day this year. Yesterday, she ____________ (read) from the book. Her English is very good. She also ____________ (teach) other students. She ____________ (write) a letter to the teacher yesterday. It ____________ (be) in perfect English. Christy ____________ (participate) in every activity, ____________ (study) at home, and ____________ (learn) new words all this year.

G. Using five of the new verbs in the past, write true sentences about you.

1. ____
2. ____
3. ____
4. ____
5. ____

UNIT 8

LESSON 2 Staying organized

GOAL ■ Organize study

A. Read about Amanda and complete the chart.

Amanda is a student at Hampton Adult School. She is good at reading and writing. She studies at home and practices writing every day. She learns her grammar and vocabulary.

Amanda doesn't go to school every day. She doesn't like to practice speaking very much. She doesn't understand English when people speak. She needs some help. She doesn't like to work in a group. She needs help with life skills, too. She doesn't go out in the community. She wants to stay home and study.

Things Amanda does well	Things Amanda needs help with
She is good at reading.	*She needs help with listening.*

B. Look at the list and check (✓) what Amanda can do to practice listening.

- ☐ Listen to the radio in English
- ☐ Watch TV in English
- ☐ Practice with other students
- ☐ Read books in English
- ☐ Look up information on the Internet
- ☐ Study a picture dictionary
- ☐ Ask questions at a supermarket
- ☐ Read a bus schedule
- ☐ Practice in her workbook
- ☐ Talk to people at the supermarket
- ☐ Read the newspaper
- ☐ Help other students
- ☐ Learn new words every day
- ☐ Talk to people at work
- ☐ Study in her book

C. Check (✓) what Amanda can do to practice speaking.

- ☐ Listen to the radio in English
- ☐ Watch TV in English
- ☐ Practice with other students
- ☐ Read books in English
- ☐ Look up information on the Internet
- ☐ Study a picture dictionary
- ☐ Come to class every day
- ☐ Read a bus schedule
- ☐ Practice in her workbook
- ☐ Talk to people at the supermarket
- ☐ Read the newspaper
- ☐ Help other students
- ☐ Learn new words every day
- ☐ Talk to people at work
- ☐ Study in her book

D. Check (✓) what Amanda can do to practice life skills.

- ☐ Listen to the radio in English
- ☐ Watch TV in English
- ☐ Practice with other students
- ☐ Read books in English
- ☐ Look up information on the Internet
- ☐ Study a picture dictionary
- ☐ Ask questions at a supermarket
- ☐ Read a bus schedule
- ☐ Practice in her workbook
- ☐ Talk to people at the supermarket
- ☐ Read the newspaper
- ☐ Help other students
- ☐ Learn new words every day
- ☐ Talk to people at work
- ☐ Study in her book

E. Read the chart.

Modal: *Can*			
Subject	***Can***	**Base verb**	**Example sentence**
I, You, He, She, It, We, They	can	read study watch help practice talk	I **can** read the newspaper. You **can** study a picture dictionary. He **can** watch TV in English. She **can** help other students. We **can** practice with other students. They **can** talk to salespeople.

F. **Write sentences about what Amanda can do to practice listening. See Exercise B.**

1. She can watch TV in English.
2. ______________________
3. ______________________

G. **Write sentences about what Amanda can do to practice speaking. See Exercise C.**

1. She can talk to people at work.
2. ______________________
3. ______________________

H. **Write sentences about what Amanda can do to practice life skills. See Exercise D.**

1. She can read a bus schedule.
2. ______________________
3. ______________________

I. **Check (✓) what you are good at (strengths).**

☐ Listening
☐ Speaking
☐ Reading
☐ Writing
☐ Life skills

J. **Check (✓) what you need help with (weaknesses).**

☐ Listening
☐ Speaking
☐ Reading
☐ Writing
☐ Life skills

UNIT 8

LESSON 3 Schools in the United States

GOAL ■ Identify learning opportunities

A. Read the chart and circle the schooling each person needs.

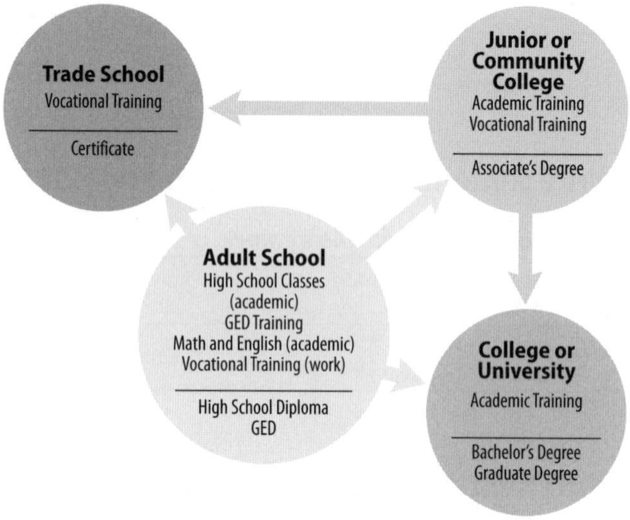

1. Marie wants to be an administrative assistant.
   High School Diploma
   Community College
   University
   Trade School

2. Gilberto wants to be a chef.
   High School Diploma
   Community College
   University
   Trade School

3. Lien wants to be an English teacher.
   High School Diploma
   Community College
   University
   Trade School

4. Mario wants to be a dentist.
   High School Diploma
   Community College
   University
   Trade School

5. Kenji wants to be a computer technician.
   High School Diploma
   Community College
   University
   Trade School

6. Anya wants to be a nurse.
   High School Diploma
   Community College
   University
   Trade School

B. Read the timeline and answer the questions.

Mario's Timeline

2018	2019	2020	2021
Go to Clear Mountain Adult School	Start a part-time job in an automobile repair shop	Go to Mountain Heights Community College and study auto repair and business	Graduate from college; start my own auto repair business

1. What kinds of schools will Mario go to? ______________________________

2. What is Mario's goal after school? ______________________________

3. When does he want to start his business? ______________________________

C. Read the timeline and answer the questions.

Silvia's Timeline

2018	2020	2022	2024
Go to Clear Mountain Adult school; get a part-time job	Get a high school diploma; start Mountain Heights Community College	Transfer to a university	Graduate from university with a Bachelor's degree and get a nursing job

1. What kinds of schools will Silvia go to? ______________________________

2. What is Silvia's goal after school? ______________________________

3. When will Silvia get a Bachelor's degree? ______________________________

D. Read the chart.

Modal: *Should*			
Subject	***Should***	**Base verb**	**Example sentence**
I, You, He, She, It, We, They	should	go attend study learn get	I **should** go to college. You **should** attend a trade school. He **should** study medicine. We **should** learn English at an adult school. They **should** get a high school diploma.

E. Complete each sentence using *should* and the correct form of the verb.

1. John and Sherry ______should go______ (go) to a trade school.
2. Kim and I ____________________ (learn) English before we get high school diplomas.
3. I ____________________ (get) a Bachelor's degree first.
4. You ____________________ (attend) a trade school and then, you will get a certificate.
5. Caroline ____________________ (study) English and then, go to college.
6. Jennie ____________________ (ask) a counselor for help.

F. Find the errors and write new sentences.

1. Gilberto shoulds visit many different restaurants.

   Gilberto should visit many different restaurants.

2. Maria should practices typing.

   ____

3. Lien and Minh should studies at a university.

   ____

4. Mario should adult school.

   ____

G. Read the information and write a sentence to give advice.

1. I am a student at Carver Adult School. I want to learn English and get a diploma. What should I do next? I want to be a mechanic. I like to work on cars.

   You should go to trade school.

2. Ivan and Gregorio are students at Emory School. They want to be doctors. It will be difficult. They need more practice in English and they need more experience in school before they go to a university. Where should they go first?

   ____

3. Roxana is completing her work at Nettle's School. She wants to be a nurse. She learned that it is not necessary to have a BA to be a nurse in her state, but she needs a certificate and an AA degree. What should she do?

   ____

4. We are students at a school in Anchorage. We all want to be school teachers. We already have high school diplomas from our countries. We need BA degrees to be teachers. Where do we go?

   ____

UNIT 8

LESSON 4 Choosing the right job

GOAL ■ Identify vocational preferences

A. Look at the job titles. Then, write the best job for the information below.

doctor	cashier	carpenter	salesperson

1. Title: *carpenter*
   Isaac: likes to work outside, likes to work with his hands
2. Title: ____________________
   Maria: has a college degree, likes to help people, wants to work in a hospital
3. Title: ____________________
   Eva: needs a part-time job, likes to count and sort money, is very honest
4. Title: ____________________
   Michael: likes to talk to people, likes to work in stores, is friendly

B. Read the charts.

Verb + Infinitive			
Subject	**Verb**	**Infinitive**	**Example sentence**
I You We They	like want need	to study to travel to work to talk to work to handle to help	I **like to study**. You **want to travel**. We **need to work** alone. They **like to talk** on the phone.
He She It	likes wants needs		He **likes to handle** money. She **wants to work** outside.

Verb + Noun			
Subject	**Verb**	**Noun**	**Example sentence**
I You We They	like want need	cars computer school books food	I **like cars**. You **want a computer**. We **need books**. They **like school**.
He She It	likes wants needs		He **likes food**. She **wants a car**.

C. Complete each sentence with the correct form of the verb.

1. Juan ___likes to work___ (like / work) outside.
2. Martin and Janet ________________ (like) computers and books.
3. Tuba ________________ (want) a new car.
4. Jennifer and I ________________ (need / talk) on the phone.
5. I ________________ (want) a new job.
6. They ________________ (like / handle) money.
7. The nurse ________________ (want / help) all her patients.
8. You ________________ (need) a job inside.

D. Read the information.

Ahmed
Likes: to work at night
Needs: 8 hours of sleep, to study English
Wants: a good job

E. Complete the chart.

Things Ahmed needs	Things Ahmed likes and wants to do
8 hours of sleep	

F. Complete the chart about you.

Things you need	Things you like and want to do

G. Read the paragraph about Janet. Then, write your own paragraph. Use *like, want,* and *need.*

My name is Janet. I like to talk to people. I like to help people. I want to be a nurse. I want to work in a hospital. I need a college education. I need to study a lot.

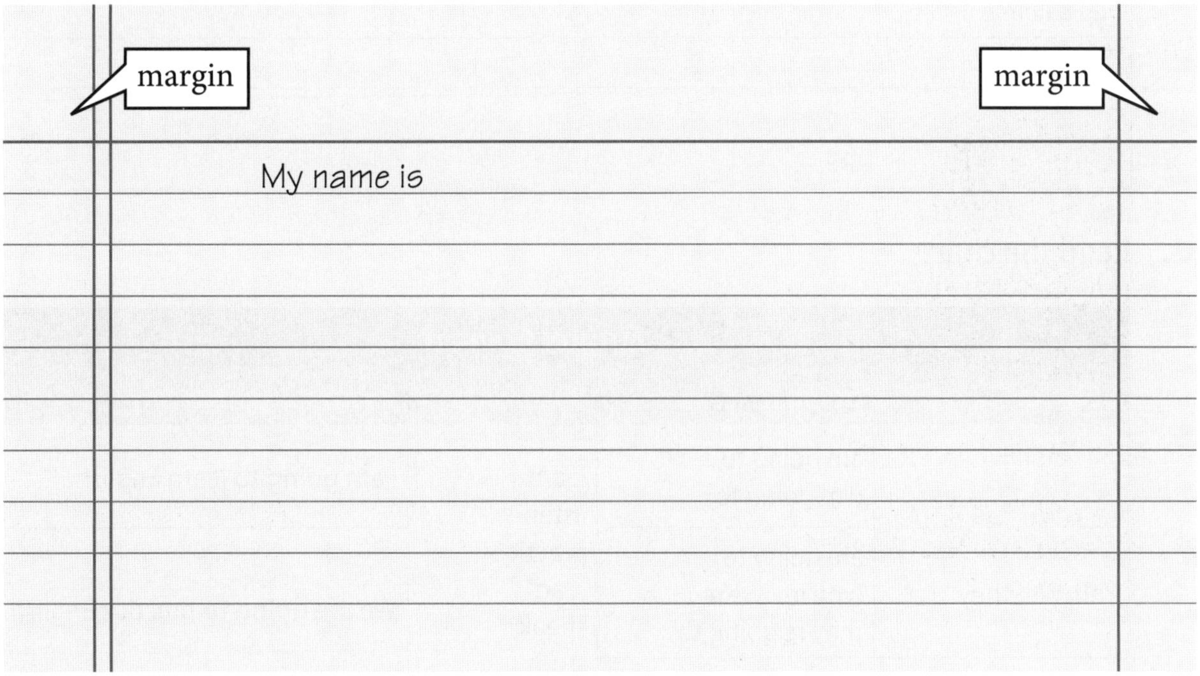

H. Look at your paragraph. Check for the information below.

- ☐ Do you have capital letters at the beginning of sentences?
- ☐ Do you have periods at the end of sentences?
- ☐ Did you write all the way to the margins?
- ☐ Did you use *like, want,* and *need*?

UNIT 8

LESSON 5 Making goals

GOAL ■ Develop goals

A. Read the goals.

buy a house	have children	move to a new house
get a good job	learn English	get a better job
get married	go to college	get a diploma

B. Complete the chart with the goals from Exercise A.

Family Goals	Educational Goals	Work Goals
buy a house		

C. Read the charts.

Future: *Going to*			
Subject	***Going to***	**Base verb**	**Example sentence**
I	am going to (I'm going to)	learn listen practice read speak study write	I **am going to** learn English.
You, We, They	are going to (you're / we're / they're going to)		We **are going to** practice English.
He, She, It	is going to (he's / she's going to)		She **is going to** study English.

Future: *Going to* (Negative)			
Subject	***Going to***	**Base verb**	**Example sentence**
I	am not going to	learn listen practice read speak	I **am not going to** learn English.
You, We, They	are not going to		They **are not going to** read English.
He, She, It	is not going to		She **is not going to** speak English.

D. Make future plans. Complete the sentences using *be* + *going to*.

1. We ______are not going______ (not / go) to a trade school.
2. Mario ____________________ (not / finish) high school this year.
3. He ____________________ (get) a Bachelor's degree.
4. I ____________________ (need) many new skills.
5. You ____________________ (like) working at night.
6. She ____________________ (talk) to the teacher about her goals.
7. They ____________________ (speak) their own language in the class.
8. We ____________________ (change) our jobs.

E. Look at the diagram of Angela and Vincent's goals.

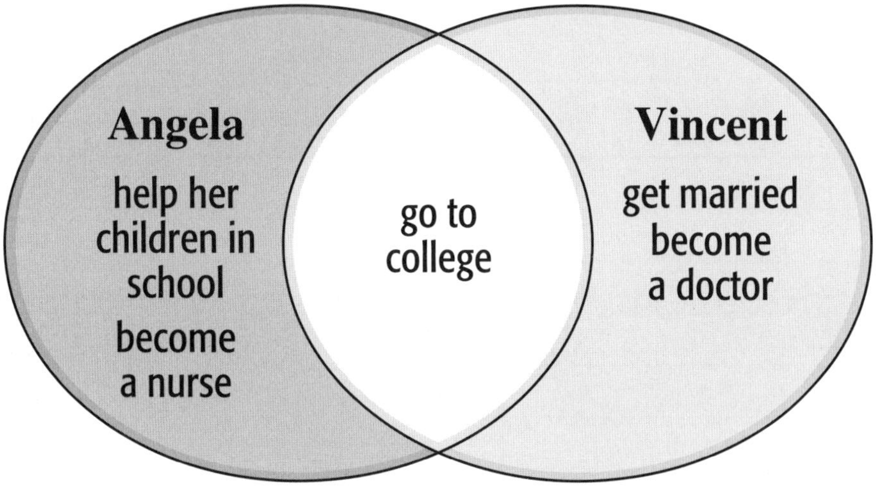

F. Write Angela and Vincent's goals using *going to*.

1. Angela is going to help her children in school______.
2. Angela ____________________.
3. Angela and Vincent ____________________.
4. Vincent ____________________.
5. Vincent ____________________.

G. Write your goals.

1. I am going to ____________________.
2. I am going to ____________________.
3. I am going to ____________________.

H. **Read the paragraph about Howard. Then, write your own paragraph.**

My name is Howard. I am a student at Alta View Adult School. I want to do many things in the future and I have many goals. I want to teach music. I am going to go to school here for three more years. Then, I am going to study at a university. I want to get a Bachelor's degree. I am going to study music. I want to be a teacher.

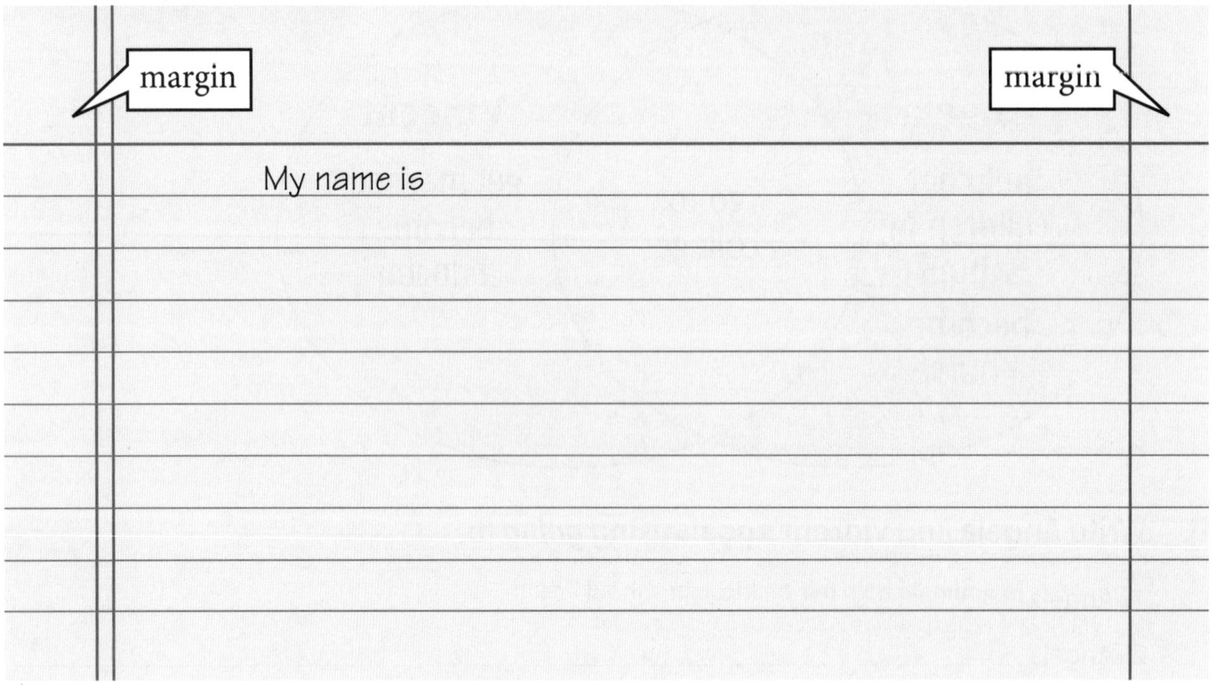

I. **Look at your paragraph. Check for the information below.**

☐ Do you have capital letters at the beginning of sentences?

☐ Do you have periods at the end of sentences?

☐ Did you write all the way to the margins?

☐ Did you use *I am going to*?

PRACTICE TEST

A. Read the diagram. Circle the correct answers.

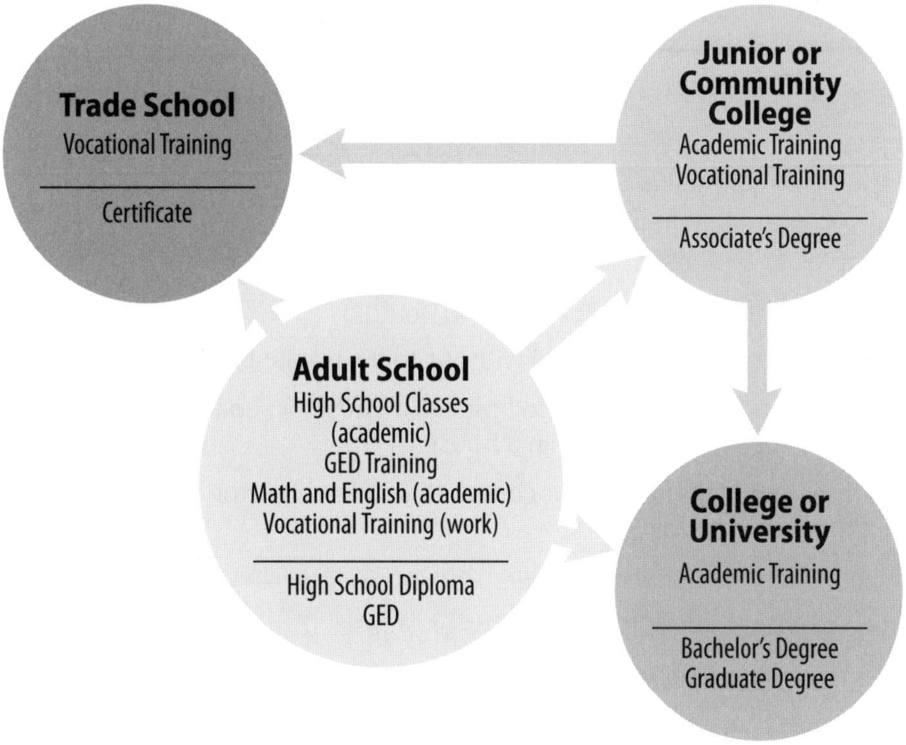

1. What is the degree or diploma for completing high school?
   a. Bachelor's Degree
   b. Associate's Degree
   c. Certificate
   d. Diploma

2. What kind of training do you receive at a junior or community college?
   a. Academic or vocational training
   b. Associate's Degree
   c. College or university
   d. Trade School

3. Where can you go after Adult School?
   a. Only a trade school
   b. Only a college
   c. Only a junior college
   d. Any school

4. What does *vocational* mean?
   a. work
   b. school
   c. GED
   d. certificate

5. What does *academic* mean?
   a. work
   b. school
   c. GED
   d. Associate's Degree

GLOSSARY OF GRAMMAR TERMS

adjective a word that describes a noun (Example: the *red hat*)

adverb a word that modifies a verb, adjective, or another adverb (Example: She eats *quickly*.)

affirmative not negative and not a question (Example: *I like him.*)

animate/inanimate objects that act or move (Example: *teacher* or *water*) / objects that don't act or move (Example: *book* or *desk*)

apostrophe a punctuation mark that shows missing letters in contractions or possession (Example: *It's* or *Jim's*)

article words used before a noun (Example: *a*, *an*, *the*)

base form the main form of the verb, used without *to* (Example: *be*, *have*, *study*)

comma the punctuation mark (,) used to indicate a pause or separation (Example: I live in an apartment, and you live in a house.)

complement a word or words that add to or complete an idea after the verb (Example: He *is happy*.)

conjugation the forms of a verb (Example: *I am*, *You are*, *We are*, *They are*, *He is*, *She is*, *It is*)

conjunction a type of word that joins other words or phrases (Example: Maria *and* Gilberto)

consonant any letter of the alphabet that is not a vowel (Example: B, C, D, F . . .)

continuous form a verb form that expresses action during time (Example: *He is shopping*.)

contraction shortening of a word, syllable, or word group by omission of a sound or letter (Example: It is = *It's*, does not = *doesn't*)

count nouns nouns that can be counted by number (Example: one *apple*, two *apples*)

definite article use of *the* when a noun is known to speaker and listener (Example: I know *the store*.)

exclamation mark a punctuation symbol marking surprise or emotion (Example: Hello!)

formal polite or respectful language (Example: *Could you please give me that?*)

future tense a verb tense used to describe actions that have not yet happened (Example: *I will study at that school next year.*)

imperative a command form of a verb (Example: *Listen!* or *Look out!*)

indefinite article *a* or *an* used before a noun when something is talked about for the first time or when *the* is too specific (Example: There's *a* new *restaurant* in town.)

infinitive the main form of a verb, usually used with *to* (Example: I like *to run* fast.)

informal friendly or casual language (Example: *Can* I have that?)

irregular verb a verb different from regular form verbs (Example: be = *am*, *are*, *is*, *was*, *were*, *being*)

modal auxiliary a verb that indicates a mood (ability, possibility, etc.) and is followed by the base form of another verb (Example: I *can read* English well.)

modifier a word or phrase that describes another (Example: a *good friend*)

negative	the opposite of affirmative (Example: She *does not like* meat.)
noun	a name of a person, place, or thing (Example: *Joe*, *England*, *bottle*)
noncount nouns	nouns impossible or difficult to count (Example: *water*, *love*, *rice*, *fire*)
object, direct	the noun or pronoun acted on by the verb (Example: I *eat oranges*.)
object pronoun	replaces the noun taking the action (Example: *Julia* is nice. I *like her*.)
past tense	a verb form used to express an action or a state in the past (Example: You *worked* yesterday.)
period	a punctuation mark of a dot ending a sentence (.)
plural	indicating more than one (Example: *pencils*, *children*)
possessive adjective	an adjective expressing possession (Example: *our car*)
preposition	a word that indicates relationship between objects (Example: *on* the *desk*)
present tense	a verb tense representing the current time, not past or future (Example: They *are* at home right now.)
pronoun	a word used in place of a noun (Example: *Ted* is 65. *He* is retired.)
question form	to ask or look for an answer (Example: *Where is my book?*)
regular verb	verb with endings that are regular and follow the rule (Example: work = *work*, *works*, *worked*, *working*)
sentence	a thought expressed in words, with a subject and verb (Example: *Julia works hard.*)
short answer	a response to a *yes/no* question, usually a subject pronoun and auxiliary verb (Example: *Yes, I am. No he doesn't.*)
singular	one object (Example: *a cat*)
statement	a sentence (Example: *The weather is rainy today.*)
subject	the noun that does the action in a sentence (Example: *The gardener works* here.)
subject pronoun	a pronoun that takes the place of a subject (Example: *John* is a student. *He* is smart.)
syllable	a part of a word as determined by vowel sounds and rhythm (Example: *ta-ble*)
tag questions	short informal questions that come at the end of a sentence in speech (Example: You like soup, *don't you?* They aren't hungry, *are they?*)
tense	the part of a verb that shows the past, present, or future time (Example: He *talked*.)
verb	word describing an action or state (Example: The boys *walk* to school; I *am* tired.)
vowels	the letters *a*, *e*, *i*, *o*, *u*, and sometimes *y*
***wh-* questions**	questions that ask for information, usually starting with *Who*, *What*, *When*, *Where*, or *Why*. (Example: *Where* do you live?) *How* is often included in this group.
***yes/no* questions**	questions that ask for an affirmative or a negative answer (Example: *Are you happy?*)

GRAMMAR REFERENCE

Simple Present: *Be*			
Subject	***Be***	**Information**	**Example sentence**
I	**am**	43 years old single from Argentina from Russia married	I **am** 43 years old. (I'**m** 43 years old.)
He She	**is**		He **is** single. (Roberto **is** single.) She **is** from Argentina.
We You They	**are**		We **are** single. You **are** married. They **are** from Russia.

Negative Simple Present: *Be*			
Subject	**Verb**	**Negative**	**Example sentence (Contractions)**
I	am	not	I **am not** in the garage. (I'**m not**)
You, We, They	are		You **are not** outside. (You'**re not**) (You **aren't**) We **are not** outside. (We'**re not**) (We **aren't**) They **are not** in the kitchen. (They'**re not**) (They **aren't**)
He, She, It	is		He **is not** in the apartment. (He'**s not**) (He **isn't**) She **is not** in the apartment. (She'**s not**) (She **isn't**) It **is not** in the living room. (It'**s not**) (It **isn't**)
	Verb	**Negative**	**Example sentence (Contractions)**
There	is	not	There **is not** a front yard. (There **isn't**)
There	are		There **are not** any flowers in the backyard. (There **aren't**)

Simple Present			
Subject	**Adverb**	**Verb**	**Example sentence**
I	always often sometimes rarely never	write	I always write postcards.
You, We, They		read	They never read the newspaper.
He, She, It		eat	He rarely eats here.

100%		50%		0%
always	often	sometimes	rarely	never

Affirmative Simple Present		
Subject	**Verb**	**Example sentence**
I, You, We, They	work	I **work**. I work inside. We **work** in an office. They **work** in a store.
He, She, It	works	He **works** outside. She **works** inside.

Negative Simple Present			
Subject	**Negative**	**Verb**	**Example sentence**
I, You, We, They	don't	work	I **don't work** outside. We **don't work** in an office. They **don't work** in a store.
He, She, It	doesn't	work	He **doesn't work** in an office. She **doesn't work** in a store.

Affirmative Simple Present: *Have*		
Subject	***Have***	**Example sentence**
I, You, We, They	have	I **have** a headache. You **have** a sore throat.
He, She, It	has	She **has** a stomachache. He **has** a fever.

Negative Simple Present: *Have*			
Subject	**Negative**	***Have***	**Example sentence**
I, You, We, They	do not (don't)	have	I don't **have** a headache. You don't **have** a sore throat.
He, She, It	does not (doesn't)	have	She doesn't **have** a stomachache. He doesn't **have** a fever.

Simple Present: *Like*		
Subject	**Verb**	**Example sentence**
I, You, We, They	like	I **like** hamburgers. You **like** french fries. We **like** fried chicken. They **like** roast beef.
He, She, It	likes	He **likes** cereal. She **likes** toast.

Negative Simple Present: *Like*				
Subject	**Negative**	**Verb**	**Noun**	**Example sentence**
I, You, We, They	don't	like	hamburgers french fries fried chicken cereal	I **don't like** hamburgers. You **don't like** french fries.
He, She	doesn't			He **doesn't like** fried chicken. She **doesn't like** cereal.

Simple Present: *Shop*		
Subject	**Verb**	**Example sentence**
I, You, We, They	shop	I **shop** for shoes at a department store. You **shop** for bread at a convenience store. We **shop** for shorts at a department store. They **shop** for books at a bookstore.
He, She, It	shops	He **shops** for shoes at a shoe store. She **shops** for dresses at a clothing store.

Simple Present: *Hurt*		
Subject	**Verb**	**Example sentence**
It My leg My arm My foot My head	hurts	My leg **hurts**. My arm **hurts**. My head **hurts**.
They My legs My arms My feet My Ears	hurt	My legs **hurt**. My feet **hurt**. My ears **hurt**.

Simple Present: *Want/Need*			
Subject	**Verb**	**Noun**	**Example sentence**
I, You, We, They	want need	a TV a book a car a shirt	I **want** a big TV. You **need** a new book.
He, She	wants needs		He **wants** a used car. She **needs** a medium shirt.

Negative Simple Present: *Want/Need*				
Subject	**Negative**	**Verb**	**Noun**	**Example sentences**
I, You, We, They	don't	want need	a TV a book a car a shirt	I **don't want** a big TV. You **don't need** a new book.
He, She	doesn't			He **doesn't want** a used car. She **doesn't need** a medium shirt.

Simple Present: *Live* and Prepositions			
Subject	**Verb**	**Preposition**	**Example sentence**
I, You, We, They	live	in at on with	I live **in** a house. You live **at** 4220 Greenburg St. We live **in** Miami. They live **on** First St.
He, She, It	lives		He lives **with** his wife. She lives **in** an apartment.

Need to			
Subject	***Need***	**Infinitive**	**Example sentence**
I, You, We, They	need	to go to drive to send to see to buy to look for	I **need to go** to the hospital. You **need to drive** to the store. We **need to send** a letter. They **need to see** the doctor.
He, She, It	needs		He **needs to buy** a book. She **needs to look for** a house.

Want to				
Subject	**Verb**	**Infinitive (*to* + base)**		**Example sentence**
I, You, We, They	want	to	run exercise walk ride do go eat sleep	I **want to run**. We **want to exercise**. They **want to walk**.
He, She, It	wants			He **wants to ride** a bicycle. She **wants to do** yard work. She **wants to go** to the gym. Oscar **wants to eat** three meals a day. Maria **wants to sleep** eight hours a night.

Verb + Infinitive			
Subject	**Verb**	**Infinitive**	**Example sentence**
I You We They	like want need	to study to travel to work to talk to work to handle to help	I **like to study**. You **want to travel**. We **need to work** alone. They **like to talk** on the phone.
He She It	likes wants needs		He **likes to handle** money. She **wants to work** outside.

Verb + Noun			
Subject	**Verb**	**Noun**	**Example sentence**
I You We They	like want need	cars computer school books food	I **like cars**. You **want a computer**. We **need books**. They **like school**.
He She It	likes wants needs		He **likes food**. She **wants a car**.

Simple Past: *Be*			
Subject	***Be***	**Information**	**Example sentence**
I, He, She, It	was	her boss friendly a cashier	I **was** her boss. He **was** friendly. She **was** a cashier.
You, We, They	were	a police officer punctual good workers	You **were** a police officer. We **were** punctual. They **were** good workers.

Negative Simple Past: *Be*			
Subject	***Be***	**Information**	**Example sentence**
I, He, She, It	was not (wasn't)	her boss friendly a cashier	I **wasn't** her boss. He **was** not friendly. She **was** not a cashier.
You, We, They	were (weren't)	a police officer punctual good workers	You **weren't** a police officer. We **were** not punctual. They **weren't** good workers.

Simple Past: Regular Verbs			
Subject	**Base + *ed***		**Example sentence**
I, You, He, She, It, We, They	cleaned	tables	I **cleaned** tables.
	cooked	hamburgers	You **cooked** hamburgers.
	prepared	breakfast	He **prepared** breakfast.
	delivered	packages	She **delivered** packages.
	counted	the money	It **counted** the money.
	helped	other workers	We **helped** other workers.
	moved	to the United States	They **moved** to the United States.

Present Continuous			
Subject	***Be***	**Base verb + *ing***	**Example sentence**
I	am	talk + *ing* read + *ing*	I **am talking** on the phone.
You, We, They	are	call + *ing*	We **are calling** for an appointment.
He, She, It	is	look + *ing* at look + *ing* for move + *ing*	She **is moving** into a new apartment.

<table>
<tr><th colspan="5">Negative Present Continuous</th></tr>
<tr><th>Subject</th><th>Be</th><th></th><th>Base verb + ing</th><th>Example sentences</th></tr>
<tr><td>I</td><td>am</td><td rowspan="3">not</td><td rowspan="3">talk + ing
read + ing
call + ing
look + ing at
look + ing for
move + ing</td><td>I am not talking on the phone.</td></tr>
<tr><td>You, We, They</td><td>are</td><td>We are not calling for an appointment.</td></tr>
<tr><td>He, She, It</td><td>is</td><td>She is not moving into a new apartment.</td></tr>
</table>

Imperatives			
Subject	**Verb**	**Information**	**Example sentence**
~~You~~	stand up		Stand up.
~~You~~	sit down		Sit down.
~~You~~	take out	a piece of paper	Take out a piece of paper.
~~You~~	open	the book	Open the book.
~~You~~	listen to	the teacher	Listen to the teacher.
~~You~~	write	your name	Write your name.
~~You~~	help	a student	Help a student.
~~You~~	read	a book	Read a book.

Future: *Will* (Affirmative)			
Subject	***Will***	**Base verb**	**Example sentence**
I, You, We, They, He, She, It	will	read study watch help practice talk	I **will** read the newspaper. You **will** study a picture dictionary. He **will** watch TV in English. She **will** help other students. We **will** practice with other students. They **will** talk to salespeople.

Future: *Will* (Negative)				
Subject	***Will***	**Negative**	**Base verb**	**Example sentence**
I, You, We, They, He, She, It	will	not	read study watch help practice talk	I **will not** read the newspaper. You **will not** study a picture dictionary. He **will not** watch TV in English. She **will not** help other students. We **will not** practice with other students. They **will not** talk to salespeople.

Affirmative	Contraction	Negative	Contraction	Base form
I **will**	I'**ll**	I **will** not	I **won't**	**go** to college next semester.
He **will** She **will** It **will**	He'**ll** She'**ll** It'**ll**	He **will** not She **will** not It **will** not	He **won't** She **won't** It **won't**	**ask** the teacher later. **need** a degree. **be** in English.
You **will** We **will** They **will**	You'**ll** We'**ll** They'**ll**	You **will** not We **will** not They **will** not	You **won't** We **won't** They **won't**	**finish** the test. **look** up words at home. **graduate** next week.
• Use *will* + base form of a verb to talk about the future.				

Modal: *Should*			
Subject	***Should***	**Base verb**	**Example sentence**
I, You, He, She, It, We, They	should	rest stay go take	You **should** rest. He **should** stay home. They **should** go to the doctor. I **should** take pain relievers. We **should** take cough syrup.

Modal: *Should* (Negative)			
Subject	***Should***	**Base verb**	**Example sentence**
I, You, He, She, It, We, They	should not (shouldn't)	drive drink go	You **shouldn't** drive and take this medicine. He **shouldn't** drink alcohol with this medicine. We **shouldn't** go out.

Wh- Questions with *Should*				
Question word	***Should***	**Subject**	**Base verb**	**Example sentence**
What When Where Who What time How long How much How many	should	I, you, he, she, it, we, they	do take go call give stay	What **should** I do? When **should** I take the medicine? Where **should** they go for help? Who **should** we call? What time **should** I take the medicine? How long **should** you stay in bed? How much medicine **should** I give her? How many tablets **should** she take?

Yes/No Questions with *Should*			
Should	**Subject**	**Base verb**	**Example question and answer**
Should	I, you, he, she, it, we, they	take call give	**Should** she take medicine? Yes, she should. **Should** I call 911? Yes, you should! **Should** they give her medicine? No, they shouldn't.

Modal: *Can* (Ability)			
Subject	***Can***	**Verb**	**Example sentence**
I, You, He, She, It, We, They	can	drive speak talk collect clean	I **can** drive a truck. You **can** speak English well. He **can** talk to customers. We **can** collect money. They **can** clean the offices.

Can (Negative)			
Subject	***Can***	**Verb**	**Example sentence**
I, You, He, She, It, We, They	cannot (can't)	drive speak talk collect clean	I **can't** drive a truck. You **can't** speak English well. He **can't** talk to customers. We **can't** collect money. They **can't** clean the offices.

Questions with *Can*			
Can	**Subject**	**Verb**	**Example questions and answers**
Can	I, you, he, she, it, we, they	type drive talk work understand cook clean	**Can** you type letters? Yes, I can. **Can** they drive a car? No they can't. **Can** she understand English? Yes, she can. **Can** I work on Saturdays? Yes, you can. **Can** he cook breakfast? No, he can't. **Can** we clean on the weekend? Yes, you can. **Can** you talk to customers? No, you can't.

Future: *Going to*			
Subject	***Going to***	**Base verb**	**Example sentence**
I	am going to (I'm going to)	learn listen practice read speak study write	I **am going to** learn English.
You, We, They	are going to (you're / we're / they're going to)		We **are going to** practice English.
He, She, It	is going to (he's / she's going to)		She **is going to** study English.

Future: *Going to* (Negative)			
Subject	***Going to***	**Base verb**	**Example sentence**
I	am not going to	learn listen practice read speak	I **am not going to** learn English.
You, We, They	are not going to		They **are not going to** read English.
He, She, It	is not going to		She **is not going to** speak English.

Possessive Adjectives	
Possession	**Possessive adjectives**
I have a daughter.	**My** daughter has red hair.
You have a brother.	**Your** brother has green eyes.
He has a mother.	**His** mother has new shoes.
She has an aunt.	**Her** aunt is from San Francisco.
We have children.	**Our** children like sports.
They have parents.	**Their** parents are from China.

Comparative Adjectives		
	Question	**Answer**
Singular	Where is ground beef cheaper?	It's cheaper at Puente Market.
Plural	Where are carrots cheaper?	They're cheaper at Food City.
	Question	**Answer**
Singular	Where is ground beef more expensive?	It's more expensive at Puente Market.
Plural	Where are carrots more expensive?	They're more expensive at Food City.

Comparing Nouns				
Subject	***Be***	**Comparative adjective**	**Noun**	**Example sentence**
Milk	is	cheaper than	juice	Milk is **cheaper than** juice.
Apples	are	cheaper than	bananas	Apples are **cheaper than** bananas.
Subject	***Be***	**Comparative adjective**	**Noun**	**Example sentence**
Juice	is	more expensive than	milk	Juice is **more expensive than** milk.
Bananas	are	more expensive than	apples	Bananas are **more expensive than** apples.

Possessive Nouns	
Possession	Possessive proper nouns
John has a mother.	**John's** mother has brown hair.
Maria has an aunt.	**Maria's** aunt is from San Francisco.
Michael and David have parents.	**Michael and David's** parents are from China.

Possession	Possessive proper nouns
John has a book.	**John's** book is new.
Maria has a pencil.	**Maria's** pencil is yellow.
Michael and David have notebooks.	**Michael and David's** notebooks are green.

Using *from . . . to . . .*				
from	Start time	*to*	End time	Example sentence
From	7:00	to	8:00	He attends school **from** 7:00 **to** 8:00.
	10:30		11:00	He reads **from** 10:30 **to** 11:00.
	5:00		7:00	He practices English **from** 5:00 **to** 7:00.
	8:00		10:00	He watches TV **from** 8:00 **to** 10:00.

How much / How many		
	Question	Answer
Noncount	**How much** milk is there?	There is one gallon of milk. There are two gallons of milk. There are three avocados.
Count	**How many** gallons of milk are there? **How many** avocados are there?	

Question words	Verb	Nouns	Example question
How much (money)	is	the milk	How much **is** the milk?
How much (money)	are	the tomatoes	How much **are** the tomatoes?

Question word	Verb	Example question	Example answer
What	is	**What** is the emergency?	There is a fire! There is an accident. A house is on fire. My father is having a heart attack.
Where	is	**Where** is the emergency?	On First Street. Here in my house. At 1432 W. Palm Street.
Who	is calling is talking is in trouble	**Who** is calling? **Who** is talking? **Who** is in trouble?	John. John. My father, Eric Ludlow.

PHOTO CREDITS

03 Blend Images - LWA/Dann Tardif/Getty Images, **04** (tl) Blend Images/Shutterstock.com, (tr) Mel Yates/Digital Vision/Getty Images, **06** (tl) Andresr/Shutterstock.com, (tr) Michael Newman/PhotoEdit, **15** Andresr/Shutterstock.com, **16** (tl) David Young-Wolff/PhotoEdit, (tc) Blend Images - John Lund/Sam Diephuis/Getty Images, (tr) David Young-Wolff/PhotoEdit, **18** (tl) David Litschel/Alamy Stock Photo, (tr) Blend Images - John Lund/Sam Diephuis/Getty Images, (cl1) Tony Freeman/PhotoEdit, (cl2) Myrleen Pearson/PhotoEdit, (cr1) Michael Newman/PhotoEdit, (cr2) Michael Newman/PhotoEdit, (bl) Myrleen Pearson/PhotoEdit, (br1) Tony Freeman/PhotoEdit, (br2) Myrleen Ferguson Cate/PhotoEdit, **19** (tl) Paul Thomas/Riser/Getty Images, (tr) Paul Thomas/Riser/Getty Images, (cl1) Hans Neleman/Stone/Getty Images, (cl2) Bill Bachmann/PhotoEdit, (cl3) David Young-Wolff/PhotoEdit, (cr1) Bikeriderlondon/Shutterstock.com, (cr2) David Hanover/The Image Bank/Getty Images, (cr3) Peter Hendrie/The Image Bank/Getty Images, (bl) Michael Newman/PhotoEdit, (br1) Mary Kate Denny/PhotoEdit, (br2) Michael Newman/PhotoEdit, **27** Andresr/Shutterstock.com, **41** (tl1) Ruslan Kudrin/Shutterstock.com, (tl2) PhotoObjects/RF, (cl) Valeriy Lebedev /Shutterstock.com, (bl) Maksim Toome/Shutterstock.com, (tr1) Buturlimov Paul/Shutterstock.com, (tr2) PhotoObjects/RF, (cr) Ollyy/Shutterstock.com, (br) Neale Cousland/Shutterstock .com, **42** (cl) Monkey Business Images/Shutterstock .com, (c) Bikeriderlondon/Shutterstock.com, (cr) Monkeybusinessimages/Getty Images, **50** Ayatgali Tuleubek/Alamy Stock Photo, **60** (tl) Baoba Images/Riser/Getty Images, (tr) Minerva Studio/iStock/Getty Images Plus/Getty Images, **61** David Young-Wolff/PhotoEdit, **104** Gorillaimages/Shutterstock.com, **130** (cl) Michael Newman/PhotoEdit, (c) Tony Freeman / PhotoEdit (cr) Michael Newman/PhotoEdit, (bl) David Young-Wolff/PhotoEdit, (bc) David Young-Wolff/PhotoEdit, (br) Blend Images - John Lund/Sam Diephuis/Getty Images, **134** David Sacks/The Image Bank/Getty Images, **135** Brand X Pictures/Photolibrary/Getty Images, **138** Vlad.georgescu/Shutterstock.com.

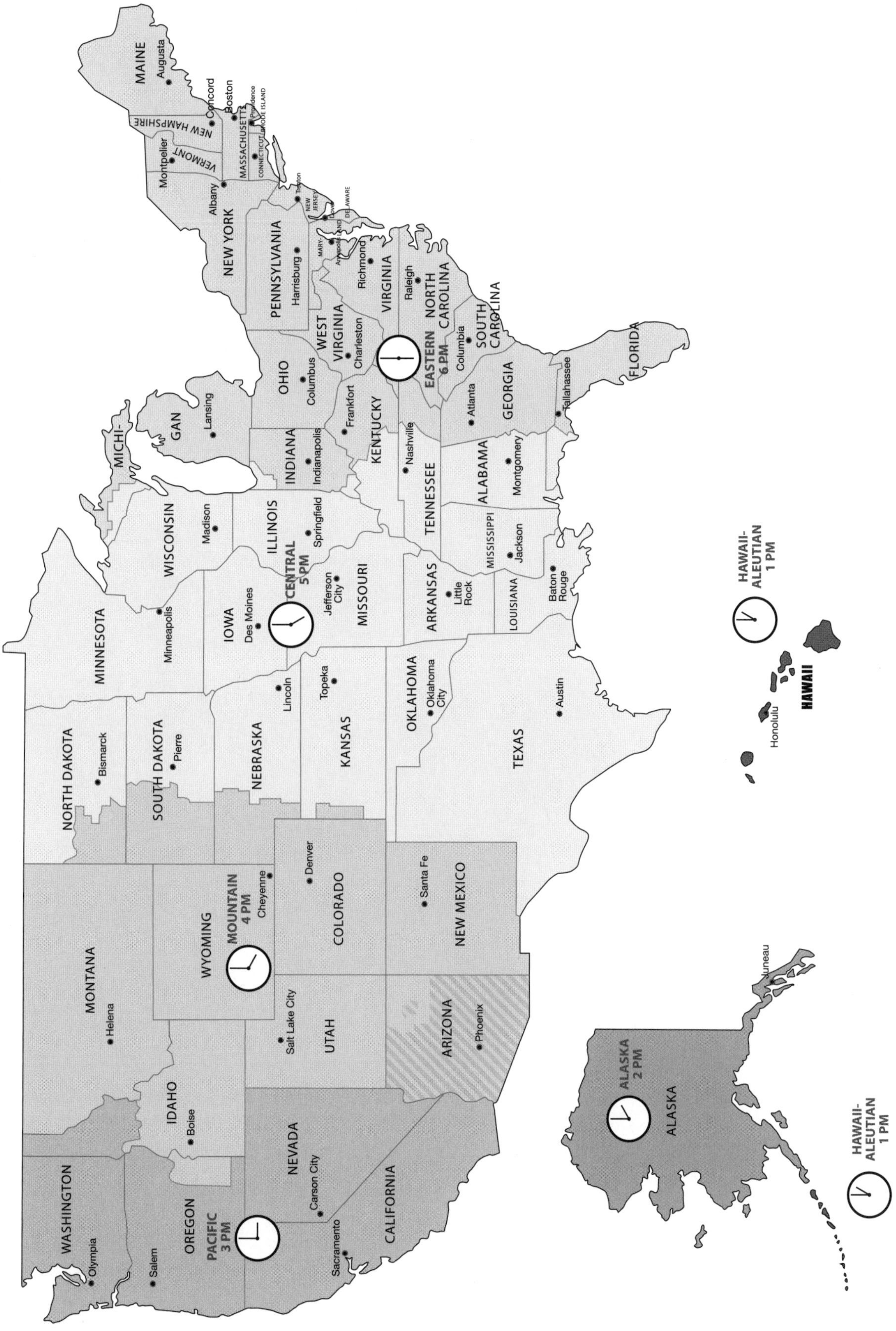

PACIFIC
3 PM
MOUNTAIN
4 PM
CENTRAL
5 PM
EASTERN
6 PM
ALASKA
2 PM
HAWAII-
ALEUTIAN
1 PM
HAWAII-
ALEUTIAN
1 PM
WASHINGTON
Olympia
OREGON
Salem
CALIFORNIA
Sacramento
NEVADA
Carson City
IDAHO
Boise
MONTANA
Helena
WYOMING
Cheyenne
UTAH
Salt Lake City
ARIZONA
Phoenix
COLORADO
Denver
NEW MEXICO
Santa Fe
NORTH DAKOTA
Bismarck
SOUTH DAKOTA
Pierre
NEBRASKA
Lincoln
KANSAS
Topeka
OKLAHOMA
Oklahoma City
TEXAS
Austin
MINNESOTA
Minneapolis
IOWA
Des Moines
MISSOURI
Jefferson City
ARKANSAS
Little Rock
LOUISIANA
Baton Rouge
WISCONSIN
Madison
ILLINOIS
Springfield
MISSISSIPPI
Jackson
TENNESSEE
Nashville
ALABAMA
Montgomery
MICHI-
GAN
Lansing
INDIANA
Indianapolis
KENTUCKY
Frankfort
OHIO
Columbus
GEORGIA
Atlanta
FLORIDA
Tallahassee
SOUTH CAROLINA
Columbia
NORTH CAROLINA
Raleigh
VIRGINIA
Richmond
WEST VIRGINIA
Charleston
PENNSYLVANIA
Harrisburg
NEW YORK
Albany
VERMONT
Montpelier
NEW HAMPSHIRE
Concord
MAINE
Augusta
MASSACHUSETTS
Boston
CONNECTICUT
RHODE ISLAND
Providence
NEW JERSEY
Trenton
DELAWARE
Dover
MARYLAND
Annapolis
ALASKA
Juneau
HAWAII
Honolulu